Savings Secrets
Insider Tips for Smart Money Saving

In a world where the price tags just keep climbing and financial worries are a daily grind, being a money-saving wizard is your ticket to peace of mind. This book, "Savings Secrets" is your trusty sidekick on this adventure. We're here to show you the ropes, share all the insider tips, and help you become a true savings superhero. Throughout these pages, you'll discover a treasure chest full of ideas, tricks, and practical advice that will change the way you handle your money. From the basics of getting into the money-saving mindset to the nitty-gritty of trimming everyday expenses, paying off pesky debt, and making savvy investments – we're going to cover it all! But we're not stopping at just pinching pennies. We're going to teach you how to set and achieve financial goals, make your budget work for you, and turn that hard-earned cash into a powerful tool for living your best life. We'll chat about everything from budgeting to the psychology of saving, and we'll get creative with ways to save big on everyday stuff. We'll also tackle big-ticket items like housing, travel, healthcare, and entertainment costs so you can have your cake and eat it too. This book is not all about scrounging and saving. We're also going to talk about making more money, planning for your golden years, and leaving a legacy for your loved ones. It's about having a life filled with opportunities and experiences that make you say, "I'm loving every moment."

As you flip through these pages, you'll gain not just financial smarts but a sense of empowerment too. You'll be the captain of your financial ship, charting your course to financial freedom with the skills and knowledge you're about to gain. Along the way, we'll share some amazing success stories, keep you motivated, and show you the path to a brighter financial future. So, grab a comfy seat, get cozy, and let's dive into the magical world of money-saving. Your journey to financial success starts now, and it's going to be one heck of a ride!

Table of Contents

In a world where the price tags just keep climbing and financial worries are a daily grind, being a money-saving wizard is your ticket to peace of mind. This book, "Savings Secrets" is your trusty sidekick on this adventure. We're here to show you the ropes, share all the insider tips, and help you become a true savings superhero. Throughout these pages, you'll discover a treasure chest full of ideas, tricks, and practical advice that will change the way you handle your money. From the basics of getting into the money-saving mindset to the nitty-gritty of trimming everyday expenses, paying off pesky debt, and making savvy investments – we're going to cover it all! But we're not stopping at just pinching pennies. We're going to teach you how to set and achieve financial goals, make your budget work for you, and turn that hard-earned cash into a powerful tool for living your best life. We'll chat about everything from budgeting to the psychology of saving, and we'll get creative with ways to save big on everyday stuff. We'll also tackle big-ticket items like housing, travel, healthcare, and entertainment costs so you can have your cake and eat it too. This book is not all about scrounging and saving. We're also going to talk about making more money, planning for your golden years, and leaving a legacy for your loved ones. It's about having a life filled with opportunities and experiences that make you say, "I'm loving every moment."

As you flip through these pages, you'll gain not just financial smarts but a sense of empowerment too. You'll be the captain of your financial ship, charting your course to financial freedom with the skills and knowledge you're about to gain. Along the way, we'll share some amazing success stories, keep you motivated, and show you the path to a brighter financial future. So, grab a comfy seat, get cozy, and let's dive into the magical world of money-saving. Your journey to financial success starts now, and it's going to be one heck of a ride!

Chapter 1: The Money-Saving Mindset

"The Money-Saving Mindset" is like having a way of thinking that helps you save money. It's about making smart choices with your money, like spending less than you earn and looking for good deals. It's also about planning for the future and being careful with your finances. So, having a money-saving mindset means you're mindful of your money and you work to make it grow and last longer.

Money-Saving is how you think about your own money. It can change as you go through life, and it can help you understand why you spend and save the way you do. This understanding can be a great tool for developing good money habits.

Here are some signs that you might be someone who regularly saves:

- Saving money is a breeze for you. You put money into your savings account every time you get paid.
- Even if you don't have a specific savings goal, you keep saving regularly because you know it might come in handy one day.
- If you won $1,000, you'd choose to save or invest it rather than spend it all.
- If you suddenly needed $2,000 for unexpected car repairs, you could dip into your savings to cover the cost without feeling a financial pinch."

Folks who are habitual savers absolutely love socking away their cash. They find joy in watching their savings grow, and saving money is a no-brainer daily habit. It's not about how much they make – it's all about having a sense of security and control over their finances. These savers usually tuck away money right when they get paid, and they're all about dividing their money into different buckets. They might not always have a specific savings goal or deadline – the idea is to save for the future, whatever that might entail. But when they do have a goal, it's usually a long-term one, like buying a house or investing.

Habitual savers are smart spenders and love a good bargain hunt. They're all about self-education when it comes to money, diving into books, podcasts, and YouTube to stay sharp. They tend to steer clear of consumer debt, except when it's part of a strategy, like racking up those sweet credit card reward points. Now, there's a catch. Habitual savers can be tough on themselves. They might feel a twinge of regret even when they dip into their savings for a necessary expense, even if it won't put them in financial hot water. Sometimes, they can go overboard with saving and not leave enough for everyday spending. Balance is key, after all.

The Psychology of Saving

"The Psychology of Saving" is like taking a closer look at why we do the things we do with our money. It's about understanding the thoughts and feelings that drive our choices when it comes to saving, spending, and making financial decisions. Think of it as peering into your own mind to uncover why you sometimes save money carefully, while at other times, you might spend it impulsively without really thinking it through.

By understanding this psychology, we can become better at managing our money. It's like having a better grasp of our own habits and tendencies when it comes to finances. This understanding can lead to making more informed and sensible choices about our money, ultimately helping us save more for the things that truly matter to us. In a way, it's like getting to know ourselves and our wallets on a deeper level, which can lead to improved financial well-being. Below we discuss some points that help us understanding Psychology of Saving.

1. Understanding Your Money Personality

Let's get real about your money personality. It's not some horoscope-type thing, but rather a way to understand why you handle money the way you do.

Your money personality is like your financial DNA. It's all about how your unique quirks and emotions influence your money habits. People come in all flavors when it comes to money. You've got:

Savers: These folks get a high from building up their savings and planning for the future

Spenders: They're all about instant gratification and don't mind parting with their cash.

Avoiders: Money matters? Nah, they'd rather stay far, far away.

Risk-Takers: These daredevils are willing to roll the dice with investments and financial gambles.

Here are some examples of each money personality type:

Savers: Sarah is the ultimate saver. She gets a thrill from watching her savings account grow. Sarah enjoys creating detailed budgets and diligently sets aside a portion of her paycheck into a savings account each month. She's saving up for a dream vacation and has a separate emergency fund just in case.

Spenders: Mark is the spontaneous spender. He can't resist the temptation to splurge on the latest gadgets, dining out at fancy restaurants, and shopping for new clothes. Mark lives for the moment and doesn't worry much about saving. He believes in enjoying life to the fullest today.

Avoiders: Laura is a money avoider. She's not interested in dealing with financial matters. Budgets and investments sound like a foreign language to her. Laura avoids checking her bank statements and doesn't think much about her long-term financial goals.

Risk-Takers: Alex is a financial risk-taker. He's always on the lookout for the next big investment opportunity. Alex doesn't mind taking chances in the stock market, and he's even invested in a few start-up businesses. He believes in high-risk, high-reward strategies to potentially grow his wealth.

These examples demonstrate how different people approach their finances based on their money personality. Each has its own way of thinking about and handling money, which can have a big impact on their financial outcomes.

Your money personality drives your spending and saving behaviors. For example, a natural saver finds it easy to squirrel away money for a rainy day, while a spender struggles because, well, YOLO. Avoiders might bury their heads in the sand when it comes to financial stuff, while risk-takers play the financial stock market like it's a casino.

Here's the kicker:

Understanding your money personality is a game-changer. It's like a financial compass pointing out why you do what you do. Once you get it, you can make smarter choices. Now, it's time to figure out where you stand on the money personality spectrum.

Look in the mirror and ask yourself, "Am I a saver, spender, avoider, or risk-taker?" Self-awareness is the name of the game. It's like seeing yourself in a financial mirror and knowing where you need to make tweaks. Once you've nailed your money personality, you can use this intel to rock your financial world. For spenders, it's about taming the shopping beast and saving more. Avoiders need to get in the money game. Risk-takers can harness that daring spirit for smart investments. And savers? Well, they're already on track for financial success. So, understanding your money personality isn't about slapping on a label; it's about embracing your unique money style and using it to your financial advantage. It's the first step to making savvy money moves, setting real-life financial goals, and crafting a strategy that works for you. And in the end, that's the path to financial awesomeness.

2. Emotional Spending - The Real Deal

Emotional spending is about spending money in response to emotional triggers instead of rational needs. Emotional spending is when you drop cash on stuff you don't really need because your emotions are calling the shots. Instead of buying the essentials, you're swiping your card or handing over your cash as a quick fix for whatever you're feeling.

Emotional spending is when you spend money in response to a time of heightened emotions, such as in times of stress or grief, and even when you're feeling happy and want to celebrate. If it goes unchecked, emotional spending can have a negative impact on your finances.

1) Exploring Emotional Triggers

Here's the thing - emotional spending can be triggered by a truckload of feelings. Stress, boredom, sadness, loneliness, anxiety – you name it.

When your emotions hit you like a freight train, you might think that a shopping spree will make it all better. Stressed from a crazy workday? You grab a treat on your way home.

Feeling alone? Maybe you go shopping to fill the void. The key here is figuring out what's pushing your spending buttons.

2) Strategies for Managing Emotions

The first step in getting a grip on emotional spending is to admit that you're an emotional spender. It's cool, we all do it from time to time. Next, you've got to recognize the emotional triggers. Why are you about to hit that "buy now" button? What's really going on? Once you've figured that out, it's time to find healthier ways to deal with those emotions. Try meditation, deep breathing, or just chat with a friend or therapist. You can also find non-financial ways to lift your spirits – take a walk, start a hobby, or hit the gym.

3) Making More Rational Financial Decisions

To stop emotional spending from trashing your budget, you've got to get serious. Set up a budget and stick to it. When you've got your spending limits in black and white, it's way harder to throw money at things you don't need. And here's a pro tip: delay gratification. When that "I want it now" feeling hits, give it some time. You might just realize you don't really need that shiny thing. Creating clear financial goals and keeping them front and center is another trick. When you've got a purpose for your money, it's way easier to resist emotional splurges. Lastly, don't be afraid to ask for help. Friends, family, or a financial guru can give you a hand when you're teetering on the edge of an emotional spending abyss.

So, understanding emotional spending is the first step to winning the battle. Take control of your emotions and make your money work for you, not the other way around. Your wallet – and your peace of mind – will thank you.

3. Delayed Gratification Or The Waiting Game

Alright, let's get straight to the point: delayed gratification is like a financial superpower. It's all about resisting the urge to satisfy your immediate desires so you can reap even sweeter rewards in the future.

1) The Role in Long-Term Saving

This concept is a heavyweight in the world of smart financial planning. It's the secret sauce that helps you make choices that set up your financial future for success. When you practice delayed gratification, you're saying "no" to instant fun (like blowing your paycheck on a fancy dinner) in favor of a bigger, juicier prize down the line (like a fat retirement fund, your dream home, or financial freedom). It's all about building wealth, making wise investments, and securing your financial well-being for the long haul.

2) Tips for Improving Self-Control and Patience

I.   Set Clear Goals

Start by figuring out what you're saving for. Having a specific goal in mind makes it easier to keep your impulses in check. Setting clear savings goals is like creating a treasure map for your money. First, think about what you want to achieve, like buying a new car, going on a vacation, or building an emergency fund. Next, make your goal specific by deciding how much money you need and when you want to reach it. Break it down into smaller steps if it's a big goal. Make sure your goal is realistic, something you can actually achieve with your income. It's like aiming for buried treasure you know you can find. And don't forget to give yourself a deadline, so you stay focused and motivated. With clear savings goals, you'll have a roadmap to guide your money and make your dreams a reality!

II.   Budget It Out

Make a budget that includes savings as a non-negotiable expense. When your money is already stashed away, you're less tempted to blow it on impulse buys. Making a budget is like planning your spending ahead of time. You figure out how much you need for important things like bills and groceries, and you also set aside some money for saving, just like a special treasure chest. When you do this, it's like hiding your savings from yourself, so you're not as tempted to spend it on things you don't really need, kind of like keeping your piggy bank out of reach. It helps you stay on track with your financial goals and avoid impulse purchases that could lead to regrets later on.

Let's say you get $500 every two weeks as your paycheck. First, you'd make a list of all your regular expenses, like rent, groceries, and bills. Let's say those add up to $400. Now, you decide to save $50 from each paycheck. That leaves you with $50 to spend on other stuff like eating out, entertainment, or shopping. When you budget it out this way, you're making sure your savings are set aside first, just like setting aside your favorite snacks before sharing the rest. It helps you avoid using the money you planned to save for things you don't really need.

III.　Automate Your Savings

Set up automatic transfers to your savings or investments. This way, you're saving before you can even think about spending.

Automating your savings is like having a helpful robot that moves your money to your savings account without you having to do anything. Imagine every time you get paid, this robot takes a portion of your money and puts it in a special savings piggy bank. It's like magic! Since you don't see that money in your regular spending account, you won't be tempted to spend it on things you don't really need. It's a smart way to make saving easy and, well, automatic!

Let's say you want to save $100 each month. You can set up an automatic transfer from your checking account to your savings account for $100 on the day you get your paycheck. This way, as soon as you're paid, that $100 is tucked away safely in your savings, just like magic! You don't have to think about it or remember to do it – it happens automatically. This makes it easier to reach your savings goal without even noticing that money is gone from your spending account. It's like having a responsible friend who helps you save without any effort on your part.

IV.   Practice Mindfulness

Be aware of your spending habits. Ask yourself if that impulse buy aligns with your long-term goals. Mindfulness can help you make more intentional choices.

Think of practicing mindfulness with your money as having your very own financial wizard by your side. This wise companion encourages you to pause before splurging on impulse purchases and ask, "Does this buy align with my bigger money dreams, like that epic vacation or a cool new car?" If the answer is "not really," you might choose to save that cash instead. Mindfulness becomes your secret weapon, helping you make spending choices that truly count and skip those that don't move you closer to your financial fairy tale endings. It's like having a guardian angel for your money!

V.   The 10-Second Rule

When the urge to spend strikes, stop for at least 10 seconds and think it over. This pause often helps you decide against the purchase. The 10-Second Rule is like a quick trick to outsmart those sneaky impulse purchases. Imagine you're in a store, and you spot something you suddenly want. Instead of grabbing it right away, you hit the brakes and wait for 10 seconds. During those seconds, you ask yourself, "Do I really need this, or is it just a spur-of-the-moment thing?" That mini-timeout often makes you realize you can live without it, saving you money and preventing those "Why did I buy this?" moments later on. It's like a little Jedi mind trick for your wallet!

VI.   Establish Rewards

Always reward yourself. Celebrate your achievements and milestones along your savings journey. Treat yourself with rewards that match your financial goals. It's like patting yourself on the back for practicing delayed gratification. Rewarding yourself is like giving yourself a high-five for being awesome with your money.

Let's say you've been saving up for a fantastic vacation, and you finally reach your goal. It's time to celebrate! You treat yourself to that dream getaway you've been eyeing. It's like saying, "Hey, I've been patient and smart about my money, and now I get to enjoy the fruits of my discipline." These rewards keep you motivated and make all that saving feel totally worth it. It's like your own personal financial victory lap!

VII.   Find Healthy Distractions

Engage in activities that take your mind off the urge to spend impulsively. Hobbies, exercise, or spending time with loved ones can be excellent distractions. Staying distracted or having a hobby or interest seems like having a secret weapon against those pesky spending impulses.

Imagine you're about to make an impulse purchase, but then you remember your awesome hobbies like playing guitar, or going for a run. Instead of buying something you don't really need, you dive into your favorite pastime, and before you know it, that spending urge has vanished. It's like your hobbies and spending time with loved ones are your trusty sidekicks, helping you defeat the impulse-buying villain and keeping your wallet safe and sound.

VIII.   Visualize Your Goals

Create a vision board or simply picture yourself reaping the rewards of achieving your financial goals. It keeps you motivated and reminds you why delayed gratification is worth it. Visualizing success is a bit like daydreaming about your financial goals but with a purpose. As a helping tool, you can create a vision board filled with pictures and quotes that represent your goals. For example, if you're saving for a tropical vacation, your vision board might feature images of white sandy beaches and crystal-clear waters. Alternatively, you can simply close your eyes and visualize yourself on that beach, feeling the warm sun on your skin. This kind of mental imagery can be a powerful motivator, reminding you why you're practicing delayed gratification and how incredible it will feel when you achieve your financial goals. It's like having a personal pep talk that keeps you on track and excited about the journey.

IX.   Seek Accountability

Share your financial goals with a trusted friend or family member. They can help you stay on track and kick impulsive spending to the curb. They can act like a wingman in your quest for smart money choices. Imagine you're out shopping, and you spot something tempting. But wait, you remember your financial goals, and your accountabili-buddy is right there with you, saying, "Hey, do you really need that?" It's like having your personal spending sidekick, keeping you accountable and reminding you of what's important. Plus, when you share your goals with someone you trust, it's like a pact to support each other in making wise money decisions. So, go ahead, team up, and conquer those financial goals together!

X.   Practice Self-Care

Take care of your physical and emotional well-being. When you're content and fulfilled, you're less likely to seek instant satisfaction through spending. It is like giving yourself a big, warm hug.

Imagine you're having a tough day, feeling stressed or just a bit low. Instead of reaching for your wallet to buy something that might cheer you up temporarily, you do something kind for yourself. It could be a relaxing bath, a walk in the park, or even curling up with a good book. It's like refilling your own happiness tank, so you don't need to rely on spending to feel better. Practicing self-care is a way to treat yourself that doesn't involve spending money, and it leaves you feeling refreshed and content.

Delayed gratification is your golden ticket to a financially brighter future. By embracing these tips and techniques, you can level up your self-control, practice patience, and score big in achieving your financial goals. It's like a financial flex that pays off – literally.

4. Overcoming the Fear of Missing Out (FOMO)

FOMO is the kind of thing that can hijack your wallet and mess with your financial peace. This Fear of Missing Out is real, and it can do some serious damage. FOMO loves to whisper in your ear, "Buy it now!" You see your friends or peers having a blast with the latest gadget, a fancy trip, or some trendy item, and boom – you're making that purchase faster than you can say "budget."

Parties, dinners, vacations – they all contribute to FOMO. You feel the pressure to keep up with the Joneses, so you splurge on social activities, even if your bank account is giving you side-eye. FOMO also turns spending into a competition. It's like a never-ending game of one-upmanship. Your neighbor gets a new car; you need a better one. Your friend travels somewhere cool; you want to top that with a more exotic destination. Money you spend to keep up with the cool crowd or chase the latest trends is money that's not going into your savings account. Your financial future takes a hit because of the FOMO spending frenzy.

Strategies for Enjoying Life Without Constantly Chasing Trends

I.   Get your financial goals in order. Whether it's an emergency fund, paying off debt, or saving for retirement, having a goal in mind helps you resist the siren call of FOMO.

II.   Second strategy is to create a realistic budget. Budgets aren't all about restrictions. They're also about fun. Allocate a portion of your income for discretionary spending, and you can enjoy life without going overboard.

III.   Be aware of what's happening when FOMO strikes. Remember, social media often shows a picture-perfect version of people's lives. You're not seeing the full story.

IV.   If Instagram or Facebook is your FOMO breeding ground, consider unfollowing accounts or muting notifications. Out of sight, out of mind, right?

V.   When the urge to spend hits, pause. Give it some time. Often, that cool thing you wanted loses its sparkle with a little distance.

VI.   Invest in experiences, not just stuff. Travel, learn, and build memories. They're often more fulfilling than material possessions.

VII.   Your friendships don't need to be centered around spending. Host a potluck, set up game nights, or enjoy low-cost activities together.

VIII.   Practice gratitude for what you have. Remind yourself of the aspects of your life that bring joy and contentment.

By tackling FOMO head-on and using these strategies, you can regain control over your spending, find greater financial security, and live a more satisfying life without constantly chasing trends.

Remember, it's your life, your rules – no FOMO allowed!

Goal Setting and Visualization

Goal setting is all about defining specific financial objectives that you want to achieve. These goals can be short-term, like saving for a vacation, or long-term, such as building a retirement fund. Setting clear financial goals helps you stay focused and motivated to save, as you have a specific target to work towards.

Vision in the context of money saving is the bigger picture or long-term financial aspiration you have. It's like the financial destination you aim to reach. Your vision could be achieving financial independence, buying a home, or retiring comfortably. Your vision guides your goal setting and provides you with a sense of purpose and direction in your financial journey. It's the "why" behind your savings goals.

1. The Importance of Setting Clear Financial Goals

Alright, let's get this straight – setting clear financial goals is like plotting a course for your money journey. It's your financial GPS, and here's why it's a must:

Motivation

Goals give you a reason to hustle. They make you say, "I'm saving for something big," which keeps you on track and away from splurges.

Clarity

Specific goals show you the way. It's not just about "saving more"; it's about "saving $10,000 for an emergency fund by the end of the year." Now that's a target you can aim for.

Measurability

Clear goals are like scorecards. You can see how far you've come and what's left. It's like turning a daunting journey into a series of small victories.

Prioritization

Goals tell your money where to go. No more random spending. With goals in place, you're less likely to blow cash on stuff that doesn't matter.

Planning

Achieving your goals isn't a lucky accident. It takes planning. You need a budget, savings habits, and maybe even some investing smarts. It all adds up to financial security.

2. Introducing Visualization Techniques - It's All in Your Mind

Visualization is a superpower for goal-crushing. Picture this: close your eyes, and in your mind's eye, see yourself reaching your goals. It's like directing your very own mental movie. The more vivid and detailed the scenes, the more you'll feel like a goal-crushing superhero. Now, think of a vision board as your ultimate goal mood board. It's your personal collage of inspiration, loaded with pictures, quotes, and little reminders of what you're chasing after. Stick it where you can't miss it – your daily dose of goal-oriented focus.

But we're not done yet — here comes the magic spell. Speak your goals into existence. If you're on a mission to pay off that pesky debt, start chanting, "I am debt-free, and I own my financial future." It's like giving yourself a pep talk in front of the financial mirror. Make it a habit, like your daily coffee fix or your weekly Netflix binge. Set aside some time, daily or weekly, to replay the movie of your success. It's like hitting the mental gym, building those commitment muscles.

Don't wait for the grand finale to break out the champagne. Every tiny step you take toward your goals is a reason to throw a little financial fiesta. Treat yourself for those hard-earned achievements, no matter how small they may seem. Life is unpredictable, like a rollercoaster. Be ready to tweak your plan if needed. Visualization is your secret weapon for staying flexible while keeping your dream alive.

So, remember, setting clear financial goals is your starting point, your guiding star. Visualization techniques are the turbo boosters that keep those goals alive and kicking in your mind. Combine the two, and you've got a powerhouse for turning your financial dreams into reality.

Time to unleash your inner goal-crushing champion – go get 'em!

3. Behavioral Economics and Saving

Let's get into the nitty-gritty of how your brain plays tricks on your saving game. Behavioral economics is like your backstage pass to understand these quirks. Two key players in this game are the "Endowment Effect" and "Loss Aversion."

1) Endowment Effect: Love What's Yours

This is a fancy way of saying that we overvalue things just because they're ours. When it comes to saving, it means you might hesitate to let go of your money or assets, even when it's the smart move. This attachment can hold you back from selling or investing wisely.

2) Loss Aversion: Fear of Losing

This one's a doozy. We hate losing more than we love winning. So, when it comes to saving, we're more likely to protect what we have rather than take risks to gain more. This can lead to super conservative investments or missed opportunities.

3) Practical Tips for Turning the Tables

Recognize the Endowment Effect: When you're clinging to your money or assets, pause and ask yourself if it serves your financial goals. Sometimes, letting go can be the better move in the long run.

Diversify Investments: To tackle loss aversion, spread your investments. Diversification reduces the fear of big losses, making it easier to invest in assets with long-term potential.

Automate Savings: Your willpower isn't always reliable. Set up automatic transfers to your savings or investments. It's like saving on autopilot.

Frame Choices Differently: Trick your brain by framing choices in terms of gains or avoiding losses. Think of saving as "protecting your financial future" rather than "cutting your spending."

Seek Professional Guidance: Financial advisors know how these biases work. They can guide you in making choices that match your long-term goals.

Set Clear Savings Goals: Having specific goals helps you fight off these biases. You know what you're saving for, and that purpose keeps you on track.

By understanding these behavioral economics principles, you can work with your brain, not against it. It's like hacking your mind for better saving and financial success. Don't let your brain be the boss; you're in charge!

3. Peer Pressure and Social Spending

Alright, let's talk about how social pressures and peer spending can seriously mess up your budget:

We've all been there, right? Your friend shows off the latest shiny tech gadget, and suddenly, you're convinced you can't live without it, even if it means your bank account goes on a diet. Then there are the social obligations. Birthdays, weddings, parties – they're all fantastic, but they can turn your wallet into a war zone. You feel this unwritten rule that says you have to show up with gifts or arrive in style.

And let's not forget about keeping up with the Joneses. The pressure to fit in or show off your status can lead to dropping some serious cash on things you don't really need. It's like buying stuff just to keep your social circle intact. Emotional spending is the sneakiest of them all. FOMO (the fear of missing out) can strike at any moment. You might find yourself impulse-buying just to join the gang or make yourself feel better emotionally.

But fret not! You can keep your financial sanity intact when facing these pressures. Always Set a Realistic Budget. Don't shy away from budgeting for social events and obligations. Allocate a portion of your income for these expenses to keep your spending in check. For example, if you have a friend's birthday coming up, you can set aside a specific amount for the gift and party expenses in your budget.

Be open with your friends and family about your financial goals and limits. Honest conversations can work wonders in relieving the pressure to overspend. Explaining to your close ones that you're on a budget can help them understand your situation and be more supportive. You don't have to say "yes" to every social event. Choose the ones that matter most to you and your wallet. Prioritizing helps you attend important events without feeling guilty about missing others.

Get creative and look for cheaper alternatives to traditional social activities. You can suggest hosting a potluck dinner instead of going to an expensive restaurant, or organize a game night at home. Explore low-cost activities or free events in your area. Take a step back and think about what truly matters to you. Building meaningful relationships and experiences often outweighs the satisfaction of owning fancy things in the long run. Your financial goals should align with your values. It's perfectly okay to say "no" politely when a social event or spending request doesn't align with your finances. Being assertive about your financial goals is a valuable skill that can help you maintain control over your money.

Surround yourself with friends who support your financial goals. Let their positive influence motivate you to stay on track. If they're also focused on saving or budgeting, it can be easier to resist external pressure. Having strong financial objectives can give you the backbone to resist peer pressure. Remind yourself that your savings contribute to your financial security and future. Whether it's building an emergency fund, paying off debt, or saving for a vacation, clear goals can help you stay focused.

Just because everyone else seems to be spending money like it's going out of style doesn't mean you have to. Make spending decisions based on what aligns with your financial goals and values. It's your financial future – own it!

Balancing your social life and your financial goals can be a bit of a juggling act, but it's absolutely doable. These strategies help you enjoy social hangouts without blowing your budget or sacrificing your financial future.

So go ahead, live your best life without the financial hangover!.

4. Coping with Financial Stress

Let's talk about the elephant in the room: financial stress. Money can be a significant source of anxiety, but there are ways to cope with it:

1) Addressing Money-Related Stress and Anxiety

The first step is acknowledging that you're stressed about money. It's okay to feel this way, and many people do. You should determine what's causing your financial stress. Is it debt, insufficient income, unexpected expenses, or a lack of financial planning?

If you need an open communication talk to someone you trust about your financial concerns. Sharing your worries can relieve the emotional burden. A budget is your financial roadmap. It helps you take control of your money, prioritize expenses, and identify areas where you can save. While making your budget, building an emergency fund provides a financial safety net for unexpected expenses, reducing stress when they occur. Financial advisors or counselors can also provide guidance on managing debt, budgeting, and long-term financial planning.

2) Stress Management Techniques

I. **Relaxation:** Practice exercises or relaxation techniques to reduce anxiety. Deep breathing, meditation, and yoga can help.

II. **Exercise:** Physical activity is a great stress reliever. It releases endorphins, which are natural mood lifters.

III. **Set Realistic Goals:** Break down your financial goals into smaller, manageable steps. Celebrate your achievements along the way.

IV. **Limit Exposure to Stressors:** If financial news or discussions trigger stress, limit your exposure. You can't control the economy, but you can control what you consume.

V. **Prioritize Self-Care:** Take care of your physical and mental well-being. Good nutrition, adequate sleep, and regular relaxation all contribute to stress management.

VI. **Stay Positive:** Maintain a positive outlook. Remember that financial stress is often temporary, and you have the ability to overcome it.

3) Resources for Seeking Financial Help

Facing financial stress is a situation that many people find themselves in, and the good news is that there's support available to help you navigate through it. You can turn to credit counseling services provided by nonprofits to get a handle on your financial difficulties. If you're looking for long-term financial planning and guidance on investments and retirement, consider reaching out to certified financial planners who can create a plan tailored to your goals.

Your local community might offer financial education programs to assist you when you're facing financial challenges. Don't forget to explore government assistance programs that can provide financial help for specific needs like housing, food, and healthcare. And always keep in mind that mental health matters, so if financial stress is taking a toll on your emotional well-being, it's perfectly okay to seek support from mental health professionals. Remember, you're not alone in this, and by addressing your financial stress head-on, reaching out for support when necessary, and practicing stress management techniques, you can regain control over your financial well-being and lighten the emotional load that money-related concerns can bring.

Setting Financial Goals

Setting financial goals means laying out clear, concrete targets for your money. It's like creating a roadmap for your finances, giving you direction and motivation to make smart financial decisions. Whether it's saving for a vacation, paying off debt, or planning for retirement, setting financial goals helps you stay on track and work towards the future you want.

1. The Importance of Setting Financial Goals

a) Let financial goals be realistic

when it comes to your finances, it's easy to wander aimlessly, hoping for the best. But here's the deal - setting clear financial goals is like plotting your course on a map. It gives you direction, purpose, and a darn good reason to make wise financial choices.

b) Motivation That Packs a Punch

Financial goals aren't just random numbers; they're your dreams in numerical form. They give you a reason to hustle and grind. Imagine wanting to take that dream vacation or own a house – that's motivation you can't buy.

c) Crystal-Clear Vision

Goals are like flashlights in the dark. They illuminate what you really want to achieve. It's not just about "saving more money" anymore; it's about "saving $10,000 for that dream trip by next year." Specific goals clarify your path.

d) Scorecard for Success

Imagine a game without a scoreboard. How would you know if you're winning? Clear financial goals are like your personal scorecard. You can measure your progress and celebrate each small victory, which keeps you accountable.

e) Money Talks, You Listen

Goals help you speak the language of your money. You start telling it where to go. No more random spending; it's all about making those dollars work for you.

f) Plan Like a Pro

Achieving financial goals isn't about luck; it's about planning. You need a budget, savings habits, and maybe even some investing smarts. It's your roadmap to financial security.

In a nutshell, setting financial goals isn't just a "nice to have" – it's a "must-have." It's the compass that guides you through the money maze. So, think about what you want, put a number on it, and let those financial goals light the way to your dreams. Your financial future will thank you for it.

1. Types of Financial Goals

Let's break it down – financial goals come in all shapes and sizes. They're like puzzle pieces that fit into different parts of your life. Here's how you can think about them:

I. Short-Term Goals (Up Close and Personal)

These are your "right around the corner" goals. We're talking about saving for that weekend getaway, paying off your credit card, or buying a new laptop. Short-term goals usually have a timeline of a few weeks to a year. They're the things you can see on the horizon.

II. Medium-Term Goals (On the Horizon)

These goals are a bit further out, like that island you can see from the shore. You might be thinking about saving for a down payment on a house, funding your child's education, or taking that dream vacation. Medium-term goals typically fall between one to five years. They're your stepping stones to bigger things.

III.   Long-Term Goals (The Big Picture)

These are the grand goals, the ones you picture when you close your eyes and dream. Buying a home, retiring in style, or achieving financial independence – these are the long-term goals. They often stretch over five years or more. These goals are your financial North Star, guiding you toward the future you want.

Each type of goal has its place in your financial plan. Short-term goals keep you on track in the day-to-day, medium-term goals help you reach a little further, and long-term goals are your destination on the horizon. It's like having a financial roadmap with markers for every step of your journey. So, what's your next stop?

2. SMART Goals

Okay, it's time to get down to business. If you're serious about reaching your financial goals, you need a plan, and that plan starts with SMART goals. What's SMART, you ask? It's an acronym that breaks down what effective goals are all about:

Specific: Your goal needs to be crystal clear. "I want to save money" is like saying you want to travel the world. Where? When? How much? Specific means nailing down the details. "I want to save $5,000 for a new car by next year" – that's specific.

Measurable: How do you know if you're making progress? Measurable goals are like yardsticks. You need numbers. "I want to pay off debt" is vague. "I want to pay off $10,000 in credit card debt in 18 months" – now you can track it.

Achievable: Your goals should be challenging but not impossible. Going from zero to millionaire in a year is probably a stretch. "I want to save $100,000 on a $40,000 salary in six months" – not achievable. "I want to save $10,000 in two years" – achievable with discipline.

Relevant: Your goals should fit into your life. "I want to save for a European vacation" might not be relevant if you're dealing with pressing debt. Your goals should match your priorities and circumstances.

Time-bound: There's power in a deadline. "Someday" often means "never." "I want to start investing" is vague. "I want to start investing with $500 per month by next month" has a timeline.

So, picture this: SMART goals are like the architect's blueprint for your financial success. They're specific, measurable, achievable, relevant, and time-bound. If you want your financial dreams to become a reality, start making your goals SMART.

3. Prioritizing Your Financial Goals

Alright, imagine you've got a plate full of financial goals, each one vying for your attention. It's like a buffet of dreams, and you can't devour everything at once. That's where prioritizing your financial goals steps in.

What's the MVP? - The first step in prioritizing is figuring out which goal is your Most Valuable Player. You've got to ask yourself, "What's the one goal that, if I achieve it, will have the most significant positive impact on my life?"

Short-Term vs. Long-Term - Consider the timeline. Short-term goals are those quick wins that can make you feel like a champ. Long-term goals are like the big jackpot. They might take longer to hit, but when you do, it's a game-changer.

Financial Health First - Think about your financial health. Goals like paying off high-interest debt and building an emergency fund usually come first. They lay the foundation for your financial stability.

Values and Passion - What truly matters to you? Your values and passions should guide your priorities. If travel is your passion, that vacation fund might move up the list.

Balance is Key - You don't want to put all your eggs in one basket. Balance your priorities. A bit of saving, a bit of investing, and some spending for enjoyment – that's a balanced financial diet.

Track and Adjust - Priorities can change. As life evolves, so do your goals. Track your progress, reevaluate your priorities, and adjust accordingly.

It's like packing for a trip. You've got limited space in your suitcase (your budget), so you need to pick the essentials that will make your journey enjoyable. Prioritizing your financial goals is your way of saying, "I know what's important, and I'm going after it." So, dig in, set your priorities, and watch your financial dreams come to life.

4. Retirement Planning and Savings Goals

You might be in the prime of your life right now, but trust me, your future self is going to thank you for this one. Retirement planning isn't just something for older folks; it's a lifelong journey, and the earlier you start, the better.

a) Why Retirement Planning Matters

Time is the best friend of your savings. The earlier you start, the more time your money has to grow. Waiting means you'll have to save more to reach the same goal. Remember that social security isn't a blank check, Relying solely on government benefits might not cut it. You want your retirement to be comfortable, not just scraping by. Retirement isn't just the end of work; it's the beginning of your time to do what you love. Whether that's travel, hobbies, or quality time with family, your savings make it possible.

b) Savings Goals

Let's break it down in simple way. First, set yourself a retirement savings goal - like, how much money you want to have when you retire. You need a clear number in mind. Second, inflation is like that sneaky money-eating monster. Your savings need to grow enough to keep up with it. Third, don't stash all your savings in one place. Mix it up with some stocks, bonds, and maybe even a bit of real estate to balance the risk. Now, here's a pro tip: high fees are like those pesky mosquitos - they can really annoy you. So, make sure your investments don't charge you too much. Life isn't set in stone; it's like a rollercoaster, and your plans need to roll with it. As you hit different stages of life, go back and tweak your retirement savings plans. Last but not least, before you go all-in on retirement, make sure you've got an emergency fund tucked away. You don't want to start your golden years with money stress from unexpected surprises.

Retirement planning is all about securing your financial future. It's your way of saying, "I want to live the life I desire even when I'm not working." So, set those retirement savings goals, start early, and let your money work for you. Your future self will thank you for it.

5. Living Life to the Fullest Without Sacrificing Your Future

Life's a journey, and your finances play a crucial role in that adventure. While saving for the future is essential, it's equally important to savor the present. Finding the right balance between short-term enjoyment and long-term security is the key to a fulfilling financial life.

1) The Yin and Yang of Financial Wellness

Short-Term Enjoyment:

This is about living in the moment, experiencing life's pleasures, and enjoying the fruits of your labor. It's the vacation you've been dreaming of, dining out with friends, or buying that gadget you've had your eye on. It's the spice that adds flavor to your daily grind.

Long-Term Security:

This is your safety net. It's about saving for retirement, building an emergency fund, and investing wisely to secure your financial future. Long-term security ensures that you won't have to worry about money when you need it most.

2) Finding the Right Balance

Prioritize Essentials:

Cover your financial basics first. Make sure you're saving for emergencies and essential long-term goals, like retirement.

Budget Wisely:

Create a budget that allocates a portion of your income to both short-term enjoyment and long-term security. Balance your spending to accommodate both.

Set Financial Goals:

Define your short-term and long-term financial goals. This clarity helps you allocate your resources effectively.

Automate Savings:

Automate contributions to your long-term savings and investments. It takes the guesswork out of saving for the future.

Mindful Spending:

Practice mindful spending. Think twice before making impulsive purchases and consider if they align with your goals.

Celebrate Milestones:

Recognize and reward yourself for achieving financial milestones. Celebrating your progress keeps you motivated.

Regular Reevaluation:

Periodically assess your financial situation and goals. As life evolves, your balance may need adjustment.

Balancing short-term enjoyment with long-term security is a bit like walking a tightrope. It's challenging, but it's also where the magic happens. You can live life to the fullest today while building a secure financial future. It's not about sacrificing one for the other; it's about finding harmony between them. So, go ahead, enjoy that dinner with friends, plan that weekend getaway, and save for your retirement. You can have your cake and eat it too - just make sure you're saving a slice for later.

6. Reviewing and Adjusting Your Financial Goals Over Time

Life is full of twists and turns, and your financial journey is no exception. You've set your financial goals, but that doesn't mean they're set in stone. Regularly reviewing and adjusting your goals is like fine-tuning your financial GPS – it keeps you on the right path.

1) Why Review Your Goals

In life circumstances change. You might get a raise, start a family, or face unexpected expenses. Your financial goals need to adapt to your current reality. As you grow, so do your dreams. What was once a far-off goal may now be within reach. Or, you might have new aspirations that need financial planning. Regular reviews ensure that you're making progress and staying accountable. It's like checking your position on the map to make sure you're heading in the right direction.

2) The Review Process

a) Decide on a regular interval for reviewing your goals. It could be monthly, quarterly, or annually – whatever works for you.

b) Assess how far you've come in achieving your goals. Are you on track? Falling behind? Ahead of schedule?

c) If circumstances have changed, don't be afraid to adjust your goals. It might mean increasing your savings rate, extending the timeline, or even revising the goal itself.

d) Recognize and celebrate your financial achievements, both big and small. It keeps you motivated and reminds you of your progress.

e) Remember the SMART criteria – goals should be Specific, Measurable, Achievable, Relevant, and Time-bound. Ensure your adjusted goals still meet these criteria.

f) A financial advisor can provide valuable insights and help you navigate changes effectively.

Your financial goals are your map to a successful financial journey. But, just like any journey, it's essential to check your course periodically. Life changes, dreams evolve, and goals may need fine-tuning. By reviewing and adjusting your financial goals over time, you ensure that you're always on the right path to financial success. It's not about starting over; it's about staying adaptable and achieving your dreams.

Overcoming Spending Habits

1. Identifying Problematic Spending Habits

Let's face it – we've all been there, those moments when our bank account seems to be on a never-ending rollercoaster ride. And it's usually because of those pesky spending habits. So, the first step to getting a handle on your finances is to pinpoint which spending habits are causing the trouble.

1) Self-Reflection – The Starting Point

Identifying Problematic Spending Habits begins with a little self-reflection. Take a moment to step back and examine your financial behavior. It's like looking in a mirror but for your spending habits. Start by asking yourself some tough questions. Are you constantly splurging on things you don't need? Are you swiping your card without a second thought? By recognizing these patterns, you're on your way to understanding which habits are tripping you up.

2) Patterns of Behavior – The Clues

Your spending habits are like breadcrumbs that lead you to the root of your financial issues. Look for patterns. Do you tend to overspend when you're stressed, bored, or trying to keep up with others? Are you frequently caught up in the allure of sales and discounts? These patterns of behavior give you valuable insight into the triggers of your spending habits.

3) Facing the Reality

Identifying problematic spending habits can be an eye-opener. It's like shining a light on the areas where you might have been in the dark. But don't worry; it's the first step toward positive change. Once you acknowledge these habits and their impact on your finances, you can start making more informed choices.

If you don't know what's causing your financial woes, you can't fix them. Identifying your problematic spending habits through self-reflection and recognizing patterns of behavior is the first courageous step to regaining control over your money. It's not always easy, but it's the gateway to better financial decisions.

2. Creating a Spending Plan

Imagine driving to an unfamiliar destination without a GPS or map. You'd be lost, right? That's what it's like managing your finances without a spending plan. But fear not, creating a spending plan is your financial GPS – it guides you toward your goals, keeps you on track, and helps you avoid financial detours.

a) The Budget Blueprint

A spending plan, often referred to as a budget, is essentially a blueprint for your financial life. It's like a financial GPS that helps you navigate your income, expenses, and savings goals.

Realistic and Achievable: Your budget should be realistic and achievable. It's not about squeezing every penny; it's about finding a balance that works for you. It's like planning a road trip with stops for sightseeing, not a non-stop sprint.

Income and Expenses: Start by listing your sources of income, whether it's your salary, side gigs, or investments. Then, detail your monthly expenses, including bills, groceries, transportation, and any other regular spending.

Savings Goals: Don't forget to allocate a portion of your income to savings goals. Whether it's an emergency fund, retirement, or a vacation fund, these are the milestones you're driving toward.

b) The Power of Allocation

One of the magical aspects of a spending plan is that it allocates your money more effectively. It tells you where every dollar should go, which can prevent impulsive purchases and keep you focused on your financial goals.

Tracking and Adjusting: A spending plan isn't set in stone. Life changes, and so should your budget. As you progress, review your plan regularly, adjust it as needed, and make sure it aligns with your financial objectives.

Peace of Mind: Having a spending plan isn't restrictive – it's liberating. It's like knowing you can afford that detour because you've planned for it. It provides peace of mind and a sense of control over your financial journey.

So, creating a spending plan is more than just numbers on a page; it's your roadmap to financial control. It helps you allocate your money effectively, steer clear of financial pitfalls, and ensures you reach your desired destinations. It's your ticket to a worry-free financial ride.

3. Mastering the Art of Smart Shopping

Impulse buying is like a stealthy financial ninja that can ambush your budget when you least expect it. But fear not, you're not defenseless. There are strategies to counteract these impulsive urges and regain control over your spending.

Think of spending limits as your financial guardrails. Before hitting the mall or browsing online stores, decide on a spending limit for that shopping trip. This limit is your boundary, your line in the sand, and you won't cross it. Having a concrete number in mind acts as a barrier against frivolous spending. It's like setting up a fence around your financial playground, so you stay in control.

You've probably heard the "power of shopping lists" before, but shopping with a list is a game-changer. It's like going into battle with a well-thought-out strategy. Create a list of what you need before you shop, and stick to it. Lists keep you focused on what you genuinely need, preventing those spur-of-the-moment purchases. It's your shield against the impulse-buying dragon.

Impulse buying often happens when you want something and want it now. But here's the secret weapon against it – delayed gratification. When you feel that impulsive urge, pause. Give it some time. Don't make the purchase immediately. Sleep on it, and if you still want it the next day, then consider it. Delaying gratification allows your logical brain to catch up with your emotional impulses. It's like having a buffer between you and your wallet.

Consider shopping with a friend or family member who can act as your financial wingman. They can help hold you accountable, provide a second opinion, and remind you of your financial goals. It's like having a co-pilot to navigate the shopping turbulence. If online shopping is your Achilles' heel, take measures to protect your budget. Remove saved payment information from online stores, so it's not a one-click process. This extra step can deter impulsive buying. And use website blockers or apps that restrict your access to online stores during designated times.

Whenever you feel the urge to make an impulsive purchase, take a step back and think about the big picture. How does this fit into your overall financial goals? Is it a need or just a want? Sometimes, zooming out and seeing the entire financial landscape can put those impulsive purchases into perspective. In the battle against impulse buying, you're not powerless. With the right strategies, you can become the master of your financial fate. Setting spending limits, using shopping lists, practicing delayed gratification, and even enlisting a shopping buddy are your tools of financial self-defense. So, the next time you feel the urge to splurge, remember your strategies and emerge victorious over impulse buying.

4. Building Financial Discipline

Financial discipline is the backbone of a stable financial life. It's about making conscious, intentional choices with your money and having the self-control to stick to your financial plan. It's not about depriving yourself; it's about achieving your financial goals and securing your future.

Think of financial goals as your financial North Star. They give you a sense of purpose and direction. When you have clear goals, you're more likely to stay disciplined. Whether it's saving for a dream vacation, paying off debt, or building an emergency fund, goals provide the motivation to make intentional choices. A budget is like your financial rulebook. It helps you allocate your income, plan your expenses, and save for your goals. By living within a budget, you're less likely to overspend impulsively. It's your blueprint for financial discipline.

So, financial discipline is like the secret sauce for a rock-solid financial life. It's not about being a money hermit; it's about making smart choices and having the willpower to stick to your money game plan. It's the path to securing your future without feeling like you're missing out.

Here's the deal: Imagine your financial goals as your guiding stars. They're what keeps you going, whether it's saving for an epic vacation, bidding farewell to debt, or creating an emergency fund. Having those clear goals is like having your very own cheerleader – they motivate you to make mindful money moves.

Now, let's talk budgets. Think of it as your financial playbook. It helps you divvy up your cash, plan your spending, and stash away moolah for your goals. With a budget, you're not running wild with your money; you're directing it where it counts. It's like having the blueprint for financial discipline right in front of you.

Don't forget to pat yourself on the back. Financial discipline is not just about saying "no" to spending, it's also about giving yourself a high-five when you hit your goals, even the small ones. Whether it's vanquishing a credit card or reaching a savings milestone, these celebrations are like fuel for your financial discipline engine.

But here's the kicker: you're not in this alone. Building financial discipline can be a rollercoaster ride. It's like having a buddy system. Share your financial goals with someone you trust – a friend, family member, or a money whiz. They'll be your backup when discipline gets a bit wobbly.

Lastly, don't forget, we're all human. We all slip up sometimes and make impulsive choices. That's life. It's all part of the learning journey. When it happens, be kind to yourself, learn from it, and get right back on track with your financial goals. Because financial discipline isn't about being perfect; it's about making progress and steering your money ship in the right direction. So keep going, you've got this!

5. Fun Without the Funds: Exploring No-Cost Adventures

Hey, we get it. Sometimes it feels like the only way to have fun is by shelling out some cash. But guess what? There are plenty of ways to have a blast without draining your bank account. It's time to explore the world of no-cost adventures.

a. Hobbies Galore

Remember that hobby you used to love but put on the back burner? Well, it's time to dust it off and give it some love. Whether it's painting, knitting, playing an instrument, or diving into DIY projects, hobbies can be a fantastic way to have a good time without spending a dime. Plus, they're great for personal growth and skill-building.

b. Go for a Stroll

Who says a leisurely walk or a hike in nature can't be an awesome way to enjoy your day? The great outdoors offers a world of adventure without a price tag. Take a walk in the park, explore a nearby trail, or simply wander around your neighborhood. Fresh air and scenic views are on the house!

c. Sweat It Out

Exercise isn't just fantastic for your health; it's also a budget-friendly way to have fun. Whether you prefer yoga, jogging, cycling, or calisthenics, working up a sweat is an excellent way to boost your mood and energy. And it doesn't cost a cent to go for a run or do some jumping jacks in your living room.

d. Quality Time

Spending time with loved ones is priceless. Invite friends or family over for a movie night, board games, or a potluck dinner. The laughter, bonding, and memories you create together are far more valuable than any expensive outing.

e. Community Events

Keep an eye out for local community events, free concerts, or art exhibitions. Many towns and cities offer no-cost or low-cost events for residents. It's a fantastic way to enjoy some culture and entertainment without breaking the bank.

f. Library Magic

Your local library is a treasure trove of free entertainment. Borrow books, audiobooks, or DVDs. Many libraries also host free events, workshops, and activities for all ages.

g. DIY Delights

Get your hands dirty with some DIY home projects. Whether it's gardening, redecorating, or home repairs, there's a certain satisfaction in creating something with your own two hands.

So, there you have it. The world is full of adventures and enjoyment that don't come with a hefty price tag. Hobbies, nature, exercise, quality time with loved ones, community events, library treasures, and DIY projects are all within reach. It's time to have fun without the funds!

6. The Power of Support

Imagine you're on a quest to achieve your financial goals and conquer those pesky spending habits. It's an admirable journey, but it doesn't have to be a solo one. Seeking support and accountability from others can be a game-changer. Here's why it's so important.

I.   Accountability Matters

Let's be honest; it's easy to slip up. We're all human, and financial temptations are around every corner. That's where accountability partners come in. When you share your goals and progress with someone you trust, you're more likely to stay on track. It's like having a cheering squad for your financial fitness journey.

II.   A Shoulder to Lean On

Life can get tough, and sticking to a budget or overcoming spending habits can be a challenge. When you have support, whether from friends, family, or a support group, you have a shoulder to lean on during those tough moments. They can offer encouragement, empathy, and a fresh perspective.

III.   Practical Advice

Two heads are often better than one, right? When you involve others in your financial journey, they can offer practical advice and insights. Maybe they've been through similar experiences or have a different way of looking at things. It's like having access to a treasure trove of financial wisdom.

IV.   Celebrating Milestones

When you reach those financial milestones, who better to celebrate with than your support system? Sharing your achievements with others makes the journey even more rewarding. It's like throwing a financial victory party with the people who've been there for you.

V.   Reducing Temptation

Let's face it; our environment plays a big role in our spending habits. When you have a support system, they can help you create an environment that's less tempting. Maybe it's choosing different hangout spots or opting for activities that don't involve spending. It's like having a team that helps you score financial goals.

VI.   Variety of Support

Your support system can come in various forms. It could be a close friend who's on a similar financial journey, a family member who provides emotional support, or even a support group where you can connect with others facing the same challenges.

In a nutshell, you don't have to carry the weight of your financial goals and spending habits alone. Seeking support and accountability from others is like having a trustworthy co-pilot on your financial journey. They're there to celebrate your victories, offer advice, and provide the encouragement you need to reach your goals. So, go ahead, share your financial dreams and watch them become a reality with a little help from your friends.

Chapter 2: Creating a Budget that Works.

Building a Budget from Scratch

So, you've decided it's time to take control of your finances and get that budget rolling. Fantastic decision!

But where do you start when you're building a budget from scratch?

Well, think of it as creating your very own money blueprint.

It's all about understanding:

- where your money is coming from,
- where it's going, and
- how to make it work for you.

Step 1: Track Your Income

First things first, you need to know how much money you have to play with. Track your income sources – that's your salary, any side gigs, freelance work, or passive income like dividends. This step is all about understanding your financial inflow.

First, take a look at all the money you're bringing in. This includes your regular job salary, any extra work you do on the side, like freelancing or a part-time gig, and any money you might get from investments, like stocks or dividends. In simple terms, it's the cash flowing into your wallet. You need to know how much you have to work with before you start managing it. That's the first step to getting a grip on your finances.

Step 2: List Your Expenses

Next, it's time to face the music and list your expenses. Start with the essentials like rent or mortgage, utilities, groceries, transportation, and debt payments. These are your must-pay bills. Then, dive into those variable expenses like dining out, entertainment, and shopping. You'll be surprised how they can add up.

Step 3: Set Clear Goals

Now comes the exciting part – setting your financial goals. What are you saving for? A vacation? Emergency fund? Paying off debt? It could be anything. Having clear goals will give your budget purpose and motivation.

Think of setting financial goals like planning a fun adventure. Let's say your goal is to go on a dream vacation to an exotic beach destination. Your goal is to save $5,000 for this trip. That's your target.

Now, you know that every month you can set aside a certain amount of money from your salary. Let's say you can save $500 per month. With your goal of $5,000 in mind, you can calculate how long it will take to reach it.

$5,000 (your goal) ÷ $500 (your monthly savings) = 10 months

So, it will take you 10 months to save enough for your vacation. With this clear goal, you're motivated to put away that $500 every month, knowing it's getting you closer to your dream beach getaway. Your financial adventure has a purpose and a happy ending on that sunny beach.

Step 4: Create Spending Categories

Break your expenses down into categories. This makes it easier to see where your money is going. For example, under "Food," you might have "Groceries" and "Dining Out." In "Transportation," there could be "Gas" and "Public Transit."

Breaking down your expenses into categories is like giving your spending a map. It helps you see exactly where your money is taking you. Think of your expenses like a big jigsaw puzzle, and each category is a piece of that puzzle. For instance, in your "Food" category, you might realize that you're spending a lot eating out at restaurants when you could save by cooking more at home. By splitting it into "Groceries" and "Dining Out," you can clearly see where your money is flowing and make decisions to spend more wisely. The "Transportation" category can be another eye-opener. You might find that you're spending quite a bit on gas and want to consider public transit or carpooling to save some bucks.

So, when you categorize your expenses, you're putting your spending under the microscope. It's like shining a light on your financial habits, which gives you the power to make smart choices and potentially save more money in the long run.

Step 5: Assign Dollar Amounts

This is the nitty-gritty part. Assign a dollar amount to each spending category. Start with your essentials like rent and utilities. Then allocate money to your financial goals and the variable spending categories. Be realistic, and don't forget to give yourself some wiggle room for unexpected expenses.

Step 6: Monitor and Adjust

Your budget isn't set in stone. It's a living document that needs attention. Regularly track your spending and see how it aligns with your budget. If you overspend in one category, adjust by cutting back in another. It's all about finding that balance. Your budget is like a roadmap for your financial journey, and like any map, it needs updates to reflect your current location. That's why it's essential to treat your budget as a living document. You wouldn't use an outdated map to navigate a new city, right?

So, keep an eye on your spending, ideally on a monthly basis. See how it aligns with the plan you've set in your budget. If you notice that you've overspent in one category, it's not the end of the world. Budgets are designed to be flexible.

Let's say you had budgeted $200 for dining out this month, but you ended up spending $250 because of a special occasion. No problem! You can adjust by cutting back in another category. Maybe spend a bit less on entertainment or shopping to balance things out. The goal is to find that financial equilibrium, where your spending matches your income and financial goals.

In essence, think of your budget as a helpful tool, not a restrictive set of rules. It's there to guide you and ensure you're making progress towards your financial goals, but it's also adaptable to life's twists and turns. So, remember to review and adjust it regularly to keep your financial journey on the right track.

Step 7: Celebrate the Wins

Budgeting isn't about deprivation; it's about managing your money wisely. Celebrate your achievements — whether it's sticking to your budget, reaching a savings goal, or paying off debt. Those small wins are part of your financial journey.

Remember, building a budget is like creating a roadmap for your financial success. It's your guide to achieving your goals and making your money work for you. It may take some time to get the hang of it, but with patience and persistence, you'll be well on your way to financial freedom. So, grab that financial compass, start tracking your money, and chart a course to your financial dreams.

Practical Example of "Building a Budget from Scratch"

Step 1: Calculate Your Income

Meet Mike, a part-time worker earning $1,200 per month. To start his budget, he takes his monthly income of $1,200.

Step 2: List Your Expenses

Mike writes down his expenses:

Rent: $500

Utilities: $100

Groceries: $200

Transportation: $80

Internet/Phone: $50

Entertainment: $70

Savings: $200

Step 3: Add Up Your Expenses

Now, he adds up his expenses: $500 + $100 + $200 + $80 + $50 + $70 + $200 = $1,200.

Step 4: Compare Income and Expenses

Mike compares his monthly income ($1,200) with his total expenses ($1,200). They match! So, he's all set and living within his means.

Step 5: Adjust as Needed

Later, Mike decides he wants to save more for an upcoming trip. He increases his savings to $300 per month. He now has to adjust his budget.

Step 6: Recalculate and Keep an Eye on It

After increasing his savings, Mike recalculates his expenses: $500 + $100 + $200 + $80 + $50 + $70 + $300 = $1,300.

Uh-oh! His expenses now total $1,300, which is $100 more than his monthly income. Mike has to make some changes. He decides to spend less on entertainment, maybe watching more movies at home and cutting back on eating out.

Step 7: Stay on Track

Now, his adjusted budget works: $500 + $100 + $200 + $80 + $50 + $50 + $300 = $1,280, which is less than his $1,300 income.

So, with a few tweaks, Mike has a budget that fits his goals and helps him stay on top of his finances. Remember, budgets are like maps for your money. They keep you headed in the right direction. Feel free to adjust your budget whenever life changes, and stay in control of your cash!

Tracking Expenses

"Tracking expenses" means keeping a detailed record or log of all the money you spend, whether it's for bills, groceries, entertainment, or anything else. This helps you see exactly where your money is going and how you're using it. Tracking expenses is like having a magnifying glass on your spending habits, allowing you to make informed decisions and manage your finances better. It's a key step in budgeting and financial planning because it helps you understand and control your cash flow.

1. Tracking Expenses: Your Financial GPS

Imagine setting out on a cross-country road trip without a map or GPS. Sounds pretty risky, right? Well, managing your finances without tracking your expenses is a bit like that. It's risky business.

Here's the deal:

tracking your expenses is the financial GPS that keeps you on the right path. It's not just about seeing where your money goes; it's about taking control of your financial destiny. Here's why it's so darn important:

Clarity is Key: When you track your expenses, you get a crystal-clear picture of where your money is going. No more wondering why your bank account is on the verge of tears at the end of the month. You'll know precisely where every dollar is headed.

Budgeting Bliss: It's nearly impossible to create a realistic budget without knowing your spending habits. Budgets aren't about restriction; they're about telling your money where to go. Tracking your expenses helps you set achievable financial goals and stay within your limits.

Spotting Trouble Early: Ever heard the phrase "nip it in the bud"? When you track expenses, you can catch any budding financial issues before they bloom into full-blown crises. Overspending in one area? You'll see it coming and can take action.

Financial Goals Galore: Whether you're saving for a dream vacation, a home, or retirement, tracking expenses is the roadmap to your goals. It's your GPS guiding you toward your financial dreams.

Spending Smarts: You'll start to think twice about that impulse purchase when you know it's getting logged. Tracking expenses makes you more mindful of your spending decisions, which can lead to wiser choices.

So, if you've ever wondered where your money disappears to each month, it's time to start tracking. It's not just about the numbers; it's about financial empowerment. It's about making your money work for you, not the other way around. So, grab that financial magnifying glass and discover the power of tracking your expenses. Your financial future will thank you for it.

2. Methods for Expense Tracking

When it comes to tracking your expenses, you've got options. It's like choosing between a trusty old map and a shiny GPS. Let's explore the methods and tools available for keeping tabs on your spending.

1. Pen-and-Paper

This is the granddaddy of expense tracking methods. It's as simple as it gets. Get yourself a notebook or a dedicated expense journal, and every time you spend, jot it down. You can create categories like "Groceries," "Entertainment," or "Transportation" and tally up your expenses at the end of the week or month. It's a straightforward way to see where your money is going.

2. Envelopes System

This method involves using envelopes to allocate cash for specific spending categories. For example, you might have an envelope for groceries, one for dining out, and another for entertainment. When the envelope is empty, you stop spending in that category. It's a tangible way to stick to a budget.

3. Digital Budgeting Apps

Welcome to the digital age of expense tracking! There's an app for everything, and budgeting is no exception. Popular apps like Mint, YNAB (You Need A Budget), and PocketGuard link to your bank accounts and credit cards, automatically categorizing your spending. They provide visual graphs and reports, making it easy to see where your money is going. Plus, they send you handy reminders to stay on budget.

4. Spreadsheets

For those who like a little DIY approach, spreadsheets can be your best friend. Excel or Google Sheets can help you create customized expense tracking templates. You get full control over your categories, data entry, and visualizing your spending. It's like having your personal financial dashboard.

5. Banking and Credit Card Apps

Many banks and credit card companies offer their apps with expense tracking features. You can see your transactions in real time, set spending limits, and receive alerts when you're approaching your budget in a specific category.

6. Cash Tracking

If you prefer cash transactions, you can use the trusty old envelope system or a simple spreadsheet to keep tabs on your cash expenses. It might take a bit more discipline, but it's doable.

7. Photos of Receipts

Some people take pictures of their receipts using their smartphones and organize them in folders based on spending categories. It's a tech-savvy way to track expenses without paper clutter.

8. Specialized Software

For business owners and freelancers, specialized accounting software like QuickBooks or FreshBooks can help you manage both personal and business expenses, making tax time a whole lot easier.

So, whether you're a pen-and-paper traditionalist or a digital enthusiast, there's a method or tool that suits your expense tracking style. The key is to find what works for you and stick with it. After all, the goal is the same: to take control of your finances and make your money work for you. Happy tracking!

3. Expense Categories

Imagine building a castle without a blueprint. Chaos, right? Well, that's how it can feel when you're trying to manage your finances without well-organized spending categories. Let's dive into how creating effective expense categories can be the blueprint for your financial castle.

a. Start with the Essentials

First, identify the non-negotiable expenses – the ones you can't skip. These are your basics like rent or mortgage, utilities, groceries, transportation, and insurance. These are the foundation of your financial castle, so make sure they're solid.

b. Break It Down

When it comes to discretionary spending, get specific. Instead of a broad "Entertainment" category, break it down into "Dining Out," "Movies and Shows," and "Hobbies." By doing this, you'll see exactly where your money is flowing, and it's easier to manage.

c. Allow for Fun

Don't forget the fun stuff! Budgets don't have to be all about restrictions. Create a category for "Entertainment" or "Personal Enjoyment." This is where you can allocate a portion of your income for things that make you happy, whether it's a spa day, video games, or a night out.

d. Savings Is Non-Negotiable

Include a category for savings or investments. Even if it's a small amount, having this category ensures you're paying yourself first. It's a crucial step toward securing your financial future.

e. Occasional Expenses

Don't forget those irregular but predictable expenses, like birthdays, holidays, or vacations. Create categories for these so you can save throughout the year and avoid financial stress when they roll around.

f. Debt Repayment

If you have debts to tackle, create a category for "Debt Repayment." This is where you allocate money to pay down credit card balances, student loans, or any other debts you might have.

g. Emergency Fund

Include an "Emergency Fund" category to build a financial safety net. Your goal is to gradually fill this category until you have three to six months' worth of living expenses.

h. Miscellaneous

For those expenses that don't fit neatly into other categories, set up a "Miscellaneous" category. It's your catch-all for those unexpected or one-off expenses.

i. Adjust as Needed

Categories should evolve with your life. If you find that a particular category is consistently underfunded, consider reallocating funds from a category where you're consistently underspending.

j. Regular Review

The key to effective categories is regular review. Sit down once a month to see how you're doing. Are you overspending in one category? Do you have extra money left over in another? Adjust accordingly.

Creating effective spending categories is like having a map for your financial journey. It keeps you on track, ensures you're covering all your financial bases, and empowers you to make informed decisions. So, grab your financial compass and start creating the blueprint for your financial castle. Your financial kingdom awaits!

4. Expense Tracking Challenges

Tracking expenses can be like navigating a winding road – it's not always smooth sailing. As you set out to gain control over your finances, you'll likely encounter a few challenges. Let's explore some common bumps in the road and how to steer your financial journey in the right direction.

If your income varies from month to month due to freelancing, seasonal work, or commission-based jobs, tracking expenses can be tricky. The solution? Create a budget based on your average monthly income. When you have a windfall month, save the extra. When it's lean, cut back on discretionary spending. Secondly Life loves to throw curveballs – a flat tire, a medical bill, or a broken appliance. These unplanned expenses can throw your budget off course. Create an "Emergency Fund" category in your budget to handle surprise costs without derailing your financial plan.

Cash transactions can also be tough to track sometimes because there's no digital record. The fix? Get into the habit of collecting receipts for every cash purchase, and later, categorize them in your budget. Alternatively, use an app to photograph and catalog each receipt. It's easy to forget that daily coffee or snack expense. But those small leaks can sink a budget. The solution is to diligently record every purchase, no matter how insignificant it may seem. Many budgeting apps allow you to set a reminder to input daily expenses. Sometimes, life gets busy, and you miss a few expenses in your tracking. Don't fret; it happens to the best of us. The key is to periodically review your bank and credit card statements to catch any missed expenses. Update your budget accordingly.

As your income increases, it's common to let your spending rise too. This phenomenon, known as lifestyle inflation, can sabotage your financial goals. Be mindful of this and continue to stick to your budget even as your income grows. Consistently tracking expenses can become monotonous. It's easy to lose motivation. Combat budget fatigue by setting achievable short-term goals and celebrating your financial victories, no matter how small.

Peer pressure to spend can be a strong influencer. If your friends or colleagues are constantly dining out, traveling, or shopping, it can be challenging to stick to your budget. Find ways to socialize without overspending, like hosting a potluck dinner or suggesting budget-friendly outings. Setting unrealistic financial goals can lead to frustration. While it's good to aim high, ensure your goals are attainable. Adjust them as needed to fit your financial reality. Some people find it hard to hold themselves accountable. Seek a financial buddy, whether a friend, family member, or an online community. Sharing your financial goals and progress with someone can provide motivation and support.

Expense tracking challenges are part and parcel of the financial journey. However, with determination, adaptability, and the right strategies, you can navigate these challenges successfully. Remember, it's not about perfection; it's about progress. So keep steering in the right direction, and your financial destination will be within reach.

5. Expense Tracking: Your Path to Financial Triumph

Expense tracking isn't just about recording numbers in a ledger or app. It's the compass that guides you towards financial success. By diligently keeping tabs on your spending, you can unlock a world of financial benefits.

1. Better Budgeting

Tracking expenses is the cornerstone of effective budgeting. It provides a clear view of where your money is going, helping you create a budget that aligns with your financial goals. With a well-structured budget, you can allocate your income wisely, avoid overspending, and save for the future.

2. Reduced Debt

Expense tracking reveals the culprits behind overspending and accumulating debt. When you know exactly where your money is flowing, it's easier to identify areas where you can cut back. This newfound awareness empowers you to make conscious choices that lead to reduced debt and financial freedom.

3. Increased Savings

A budget born from expense tracking isn't just about reining in spending; it's also about boosting your savings. You can set specific savings goals and allocate funds accordingly. Whether it's an emergency fund, a dream vacation, or retirement savings, tracking expenses helps you reach those milestones.

4. Financial Well-Being

Your financial well-being isn't just about numbers on a statement; it's about peace of mind. Expense tracking contributes to this sense of financial security by helping you stay in control. You won't be haunted by uncertainties about your financial future because you'll have a plan in place.

5. Informed Decision-Making

Armed with a clear understanding of your spending habits, you can make informed financial decisions. Should you invest in a particular opportunity? Can you afford a major purchase? Expense tracking provides the data you need to answer these questions confidently.

6. Reduced Stress

Financial stress often arises from not knowing where your money is going or constantly worrying about bills. Expense tracking can alleviate this stress by giving you a sense of control and predictability. You'll know exactly when and where your money needs to go.

7. Improved Financial Habits

Expense tracking isn't just a tool for today; it's an instrument for building lifelong financial habits. Over time, tracking expenses becomes second nature, helping you maintain your financial health and continue growing your wealth.

8. Goal Achievement

Setting and achieving financial goals is a rewarding experience. Expense tracking fuels goal achievement by providing the discipline and visibility needed to stay on track. As you reach each milestone, you'll gain confidence and motivation to pursue bigger goals.

9. Lifestyle Alignment

Tracking expenses helps you ensure that your spending aligns with your values and priorities. You'll make financial decisions that reflect what's truly important to you, fostering a sense of fulfillment and contentment.

Expense tracking isn't just a chore; it's a path to financial triumph. It empowers you to take control of your finances, reduce debt, save for the future, and ultimately achieve the financial well-being you desire. It's not just about watching your money; it's about making your money work for you. So, let's track those expenses and embark on a journey to financial success!

Identifying Non-Essential Spending

"Identifying non-essential spending" means recognizing and separating your expenses into two categories:

- things you truly need (essential) and
- things that are more like wants or nice-to-haves (non-essential).

Essential spending covers things like housing, food, transportation, and basic utilities, while non-essential spending includes items or activities that aren't necessary for your basic well-being. It's about distinguishing between what's crucial for your daily life and what you can cut back on or eliminate to save money and meet your financial goals.

1. Essential vs. Non-Essential Expenses

In the world of budgeting and expense management, one of the first steps is distinguishing between essential and non-essential expenses. It's a line that can significantly impact your financial well-being. Let's break it down.

a) Essential Expenses

These are the non-negotiables, the things you need to live and maintain your well-being. Think housing (rent or mortgage), utilities (electricity, water, gas), groceries, and transportation to work. Essential expenses are the pillars of your financial life, and they deserve your first attention.

b) Non-Essential Expenses

Non-essentials are the extra comforts and conveniences that enhance your life but aren't absolutely required. Dining out, entertainment, shopping for non-essential items, and subscription services fall into this category.

c) Drawing the Line

The key to successful budgeting is drawing a clear line between these two categories. While it may seem simple, it's often where people stumble. Sometimes, non-essential expenses sneakily disguise themselves as essential. That daily latte or impulse buy might feel essential, but in reality, they're non-essential expenses that can add up quickly.

d) Prioritization

The essence of this distinction is prioritization. Essential expenses get paid first. They secure your fundamental needs. Non-essentials come afterward, and they're funded with what's left over. This practice ensures that your financial foundation remains strong.

e) A Balancing Act

It's important to note that non-essentials aren't the enemy. Life should be enjoyable, and non-essentials provide comfort, enjoyment, and relaxation. The key is finding a balance that aligns with your financial goals. This might mean cutting back on non-essentials when needed or finding more cost-effective ways to enjoy them.

f) Discipline and Flexibility

Distinguishing between essential and non-essential expenses requires discipline. It also calls for adaptability. Life can throw curveballs, and your budget should be flexible enough to handle them. Sometimes, a non-essential expense may need to become essential temporarily.

g) Review and Reflect

Regularly review your expenses to ensure that you're keeping the line between essential and non-essential spending clear. This practice will help you make informed financial choices and work towards your financial goals with confidence.

Distinguishing between essential and non-essential expenses is the cornerstone of sound financial management. It ensures your financial foundation is solid while allowing you to enjoy the finer things in life without sacrificing your long-term financial well-being. It's about striking that balance that works for you and your financial goals.

2. Lifestyle Inflation

Lifestyle inflation, often referred to as "lifestyle creep," is a sneaky financial phenomenon that can quietly erode your financial progress. It's when your expenses gradually increase as your income rises, causing you to maintain or even expand your spending as your earnings grow. Here's how to identify and manage it.

I.   Recognizing the Signs

Lifestyle inflation often starts with small, subtle changes in your spending habits. Maybe you begin dining out more frequently, upgrading your vehicle, or splurging on the latest gadgets as your paycheck increases. At first, these changes might seem harmless, but over time, they can accumulate into significant financial strain.

II.   Assessing Your Financial Progress

Take a moment to evaluate your financial journey. Have your expenses steadily increased alongside your income? Lifestyle inflation can make it challenging to save, invest, or pay down debt because it consumes a larger portion of your income.

III.   Reevaluating Your Priorities

Consider your long-term financial goals. Are you on track to achieve them, or has lifestyle inflation been diverting your resources away from savings and investments? Lifestyle inflation can lead to a cycle where you consistently feel the need to earn more to maintain your lifestyle, making it harder to attain your financial objectives.

IV.   Setting Boundaries

To combat lifestyle inflation, establish boundaries for your spending. When your income increases, don't immediately allocate the extra funds to non-essential expenses. Instead, consider directing the additional income towards savings, investments, or debt reduction to ensure your financial future remains secure.

V.   Practice Gratitude

Recognize and appreciate the comforts you already enjoy. Often, lifestyle inflation is driven by a desire for more without fully appreciating what you currently have. Practicing gratitude can help you find contentment in your present circumstances, reducing the temptation to inflate your lifestyle.

VI.   Regularly Review Your Budget

Periodically review your budget to assess your spending patterns. Make sure your budget aligns with your financial goals and that any increases in spending are intentional, not a result of unconscious lifestyle inflation.

VII.   Invest in Your Future

When your income rises, consider allocating a significant portion of the extra money towards investments, retirement savings, or debt reduction. By making financial growth a priority, you can prevent lifestyle inflation from derailing your long-term financial success.

VIII.   Reevaluate Your Purchases

Before making a significant purchase, take a moment to consider its long-term impact on your finances. Will this expense contribute to your well-being, or is it simply a product of lifestyle inflation? This reflection can help you make more conscious spending decisions.

IX.   Seek Balance

Finding a balance between enjoying your hard-earned income and maintaining financial responsibility is key. Lifestyle inflation doesn't mean you can't enjoy life; it means being mindful of the choices you make with your increased income.

Lifestyle inflation can be subtle, but its consequences can be profound. By identifying the signs, reevaluating your priorities, and practicing conscious spending, you can keep it in check and continue on the path to financial success.

3. Taming Impulse Purchases

Impulse purchases, those spur-of-the-moment buys that often leave you with buyer's remorse, can take a toll on your finances. Recognizing them is the first step in taking control. Here's how to identify and tame impulse buying.

Sudden, Unplanned Spending

Impulse purchases are characterized by their spontaneity. You didn't plan to buy that item; you just stumbled upon it and felt an overwhelming urge to own it. If you often find yourself making unplanned buys, you may have an impulse buying habit.

Emotional Triggers

Emotions play a significant role in impulse buying. You might make these purchases when you're feeling stressed, bored, lonely, or even happy. Identifying the emotions that trigger your urge to buy can help you recognize and manage this behavior.

Lack of Need or Purpose

Impulse purchases are typically items you didn't need or had no specific purpose for. If you're buying things just because they're on sale or because they caught your eye, it's likely an impulse buy.

Frequent Small Expenses

Impulse buying can add up over time, even if each individual purchase is small. If you find that you're making frequent small purchases, like daily coffee or snacks, it's worth examining if they're impulsive in nature.

Post-Purchase Regret

Do you often feel regret or guilt after making a purchase? This is a strong sign of impulse buying. You bought something without thoroughly considering the consequences.

Lack of Research

Impulse purchases typically happen without prior research or comparison shopping. You see it, you want it, you buy it. If you skip the research phase and dive into a purchase, it's likely impulsive.

Unplanned Expenses in Your Budget

When you're reviewing your monthly budget, if you notice a category for unplanned or impulse expenses, it's a clear indication that you've been engaging in impulse buying.

The "Just-In-Case" Mentality

Sometimes, impulse buying can be driven by a fear of missing out. You might think, "I might need this someday," and make a purchase. If this mentality is a frequent occurrence, it's a sign of impulse buying.

Compulsive Online Shopping

The ease of online shopping has made impulse buying more prevalent. If you often find yourself browsing online stores and making unplanned purchases, it's a sign of impulsive spending.

Frequent Clearance Rack Visits

If you're constantly drawn to clearance racks or sales, it can indicate an impulse buying habit. These bargains can lead to purchases you didn't originally intend to make.

Recognizing is the First Step

Identifying impulse purchases is the crucial first step in regaining control over your spending. It's about becoming more mindful of your buying habits and understanding the triggers that lead to impulsive decisions.

Curbing Impulse Buying

Once you've identified your impulse buying tendencies, you can work on strategies to curb them. This might involve setting a spending limit, creating a shopping list, or practicing delayed gratification. By becoming a more conscious consumer, you can protect your finances and make purchases that truly align with your needs and values.

4. Subscription Overload

In today's digital age, it's easy to fall victim to what's known as "subscription overload." This term refers to the accumulation of numerous subscription services, from streaming platforms and magazines to gym memberships and more. Managing these subscriptions can become a financial drain if not handled carefully.

Here's how to recognize and tackle subscription overload.

1. The first step in dealing with subscription overload is to conduct regular reviews. This can be done monthly or quarterly. Look through your bank or credit card statements and make a list of every subscription you're paying for.

2. As you review your subscriptions, consider each one's value in your life. Are you actively using and benefiting from it? If a subscription no longer serves a purpose or brings you joy, it may be time to consider canceling it.

3. Calculate the total monthly and yearly cost of all your subscriptions. This can be an eye-opening exercise, showing you how much money you're dedicating to these services. Knowing the financial impact is crucial for deciding which subscriptions to keep and which to let go.

4. Once you've identified your subscriptions and their costs, prioritize them based on their importance and relevance to your life. For instance, healthcare or essential business-related subscriptions should be higher on your list than entertainment services.

5. Consider setting a specific budget for subscriptions within your overall budget. This ensures that your subscriptions remain manageable and don't overshadow other financial priorities.

6. If you share living space with others, explore the possibility of sharing certain subscriptions to cut costs. Many streaming platforms, for example, offer multiple user profiles, allowing you to share the service with family members.

7. Be cautious about free trial offers. They often lead to paid subscriptions if you don't cancel in time. Keep a calendar reminder to cancel trial subscriptions if they don't provide sufficient value.

8. Some providers offer bundle deals, allowing you to access multiple services at a reduced price. This can be a cost-effective way to enjoy your favorite content.

9. When you decide to cancel a subscription, set a reminder or automate the cancellation process if the option is available. This reduces the risk of forgetting and incurring unnecessary costs.

10. Before committing to new subscriptions, evaluate their long-term value. Ask yourself if you'll genuinely benefit from the service. Avoid subscribing to new services on impulse.

11. Make it a habit to conduct an annual subscription review. It's an effective way to ensure that you're not accumulating subscriptions you no longer need or use.

Tackling subscription overload is not just about saving money; it's about prioritizing your financial well-being. By managing your subscriptions mindfully, you can ensure that your hard-earned money goes towards services that genuinely enhance your life while reducing the burden of unnecessary expenses.

5. Regain Control of Your Food Budget

Dining out and ordering takeout have become an integral part of modern life, offering convenience and enjoyment. However, these expenses can quickly spiral out of control, wreaking havoc on your budget. To avoid financial strain and regain control of your food spending, you need a strategic approach.

Setting a budget is the first and most crucial step. Determine a reasonable monthly allocation specifically for dining out and takeout. This budget should harmonize with your overall financial goals, allowing you to enjoy these treats without endangering your financial health. Having a set limit forces you to make conscious choices and prevents mindless spending.

Meal planning is your ally in this endeavor. By mapping out your weekly meals, including both homemade and dine-out options, you gain structure and clarity. Decide which occasions are reserved for dining out, and which are better suited for homemade meals. Having a plan not only helps you save money but also reduces the likelihood of impulsive spending.

Cooking at home is a powerful strategy. Preparing your meals not only stretches your budget but also grants you control over ingredients and portions. It's an opportunity to savor the creative process of cooking and experiment with diverse cuisines. The money saved through cooking at home can be allocated to other financial goals.

While dining out, prioritize affordable options. Look for restaurants offering early bird specials, happy hour discounts, or deals on certain days of the week. You can still relish restaurant meals without breaking the bank by selecting places that are budget-friendly.

Reducing the frequency of dining out and takeout is another effective tactic. It transforms these activities into occasional treats rather than regular habits. By doing so, you can appreciate them even more when they occur, all while fortifying your budget.

Sharing meals when dining out is a double win. It not only fosters a communal dining experience but also reduces individual costs. If the restaurant's portion sizes are generous, consider splitting dishes with dining companions. Bringing your lunch to work or school is a practical habit. It not only reduces your food expenses but also allows you to have healthier, customized meals. Planning and preparing your lunches is a cost-effective measure that prevents impulsive takeout orders.

Adopting a cash-only approach when dining out is a strategic move to limit your spending. By leaving your credit or debit card at home and taking only the allocated cash for the meal, you create a built-in safeguard against exceeding your budget. Restaurant loyalty programs and coupons are valuable tools for savings. Many eateries offer rewards, discounts, or complimentary items for frequent customers. These incentives can significantly reduce your overall dining expenses.

Opting for cost-effective beverages, such as water or other non-alcoholic options, instead of pricier drinks like sodas or alcoholic beverages can keep your dining expenses in check. Beverages often constitute a substantial portion of the final bill, so making frugal choices can lead to significant savings. Skip appetizers and desserts when dining out, as these extras tend to be more expensive than the main dishes. By omitting them, you can still enjoy a satisfying meal while keeping your expenses under control.

Don't let uneaten food go to waste. If your restaurant portion is larger than you can finish, request a takeout container to bring leftovers home. Enjoying these leftovers as a meal the next day minimizes food waste and maximizes your dining out expenses. Finally, it's essential to maintain diligent expense tracking. Keep a record of your dining out and takeout expenditures and review your spending periodically. This practice helps you identify areas where further adjustments can be made, ensuring you stay within your budget.

By implementing these strategies and maintaining a balanced approach, you can continue to enjoy dining out and takeout while keeping your finances in good shape. It's about creating a lifestyle that allows you to savor these experiences without compromising your financial well-being.

6. Reclaim Control Over Your Spending

Let's talk about how our shopping habits can totally mess with our cash flow. You ever get to the end of the month and wonder where the heck all your hard-earned money disappeared to? It's like it vanished into thin air, right? Well, that's often thanks to our sneaky discretionary shopping habits. So, what's discretionary shopping, you ask? It's all about those impulse buys, the constant craving for the newest stuff, whether it's the latest tech gadgets, fashion goodies, or just random things you don't really need. Sure, it can be fun to indulge in some retail therapy, but it can seriously wreck your budget and mess with your financial well-being.

you can totally take control of this spending madness. First step, look in the mirror (not literally, though). It's all about self-reflection. Take an honest peek at your shopping habits. Are you the impulsive type, especially when stressed or feeling all the feels? Identifying these patterns is like shining a spotlight on your spending triggers, which makes it way easier to make some changes.

Now, let's talk about feelings. Yep, emotions are a big trigger for spending. Stress, boredom, sadness – you name it. When you're aware of what's making you reach for your wallet, you can develop some strategies to deal with those feelings in healthier ways. For instance, instead of hitting the mall when stressed, maybe try some meditation or yoga for a change.

Here's a hot tip: set some clear financial goals. Having specific targets, like building an emergency fund, paying off debt, or saving for a dream vacation, gives you a sense of purpose and focus. It shifts your mindset from impulsive buying to being smart about your money and reaching those goals.

And, you can't forget the good ol' budget. It's like your money GPS, showing you where your cash is going. Create a budget with your income, essential expenses, savings goals, and a category for discretionary spending. By setting a limit for your impulse buys and actually sticking to it, you can stop those unplanned shopping sprees.

Let's talk delayed gratification. When you feel that urge to splurge, take a breath and think it over. It's like a shopping time-out. This pause helps you decide if you really need that item or if it's just a fleeting desire. Most times, you'll realize the urge fades, and you'll make more thoughtful choices. Here's the deal: prioritize your spending. Cover your needs first, like rent and groceries. Then, focus on savings and financial goals. Discretionary spending comes last on the list, so you're looking after the important stuff first.

Mindful shopping is a slick move too. Before swiping that card, ask yourself if the purchase serves a real purpose or brings you genuine joy. Does it fit your financial goals? This kind of awareness leads to smarter choices and less spending on random stuff. If those tempting email newsletters and social media ads keep getting you in trouble, unsubscribe! Less exposure to shopping temptations can help you stay on track with your money goals. Think about setting spending limits for different categories of impulse purchases. You know, like a monthly cap on clothes, entertainment, or eating out. When you stick to these limits, you stay in control. Embrace a minimalist mindset. It's all about quality over quantity. Focus on cherishing what you have rather than accumulating more stuff. Declutter and simplify your life.

And last but not least, find joy in non-spending activities. Hobbies, exercise, volunteering, or hanging out with loved ones – these things can make you happy without draining your wallet. And here's a big one: be grateful for what you've got. Regularly remind yourself of the things that bring you joy. It can help curb that never-ending craving for more stuff and lead to a more content life. So, tackle those discretionary shopping habits by being aware, making a plan, and making wiser choices. It's your path to financial empowerment and a more intentional approach to spending. You got this!

7. Art of Managing Entertainment and Leisure Spending

We all love to have a good time, kick back, and enjoy life, whether it's catching a movie, dining out with friends, or planning a weekend getaway. However, the cost of leisure activities and entertainment can sometimes put a strain on our wallets. Here, we'll delve into practical tips and strategies for managing your entertainment and leisure spending without feeling like you're missing out on the fun.

Prioritize Your Pleasures

First things first, let's get your priorities straight. It's crucial to decide what leisure activities matter most to you. Is it those live concerts or the weekend brunches with friends? Knowing your top picks helps you allocate your money where it matters most, so you can savor every moment without guilt.

Budget Like a Pro

Creating a designated entertainment budget is a must. This budget should cover all your leisure adventures, from sports events to weekend getaways. By assigning a specific chunk of your income to these experiences, you can enjoy them guilt-free without threatening your financial stability.

Hunt for Deals and Discounts

Never underestimate the power of a good deal or a discount. Plenty of entertainment venues and leisure activities offer special promotions, coupons, or loyalty programs. Utilize them to your advantage and save some cash for extra popcorn at the movies.

Plan Ahead for Savings

Planning your entertainment in advance can be a money-saver. Consider booking your flights well ahead of your vacation, or snag those event tickets during early bird sales. A little bit of planning can go a long way in cutting your expenses.

Keep an Eye on Free and Low-Cost Fun

Don't forget the joy of free or low-cost activities. Hiking, picnics, free community events, and cultural outings often provide fantastic experiences without the hefty price tag.

Set Spending Limits and Stick to Them

You're the boss of your budget, so set spending limits for various entertainment and leisure categories. Whether it's nights out with friends, concerts, or dining, clearly defined limits help you keep a lid on your spending.

Learn the Art of Frugality

Frugality can be your best friend when it comes to managing leisure expenses. Focus on squeezing every drop of joy out of your experiences rather than the price tag. Whether it's a game night with friends or a free local event, find happiness in the little things.

Share the Fun (and the Costs)

Leisure activities can often be more budget-friendly when shared with friends or family. Consider splitting expenses, whether it's accommodations for a trip or the bill at a restaurant. Group activities can equal big savings.

Review Your Subscriptions

Take a good look at your subscription services. From streaming platforms to gym memberships, those monthly charges can add up. If you're not making the most of these services, it might be time to cut some loose and free up some cash for other meaningful experiences.

Track Your Spending

Keep tabs on your expenses using a budgeting app or software. Regularly monitoring your spending provides valuable insights into where your leisure money is going. This awareness helps you make informed decisions about where to cut back or redirect funds.

Set Those Goals

Finally, link your leisure and entertainment spending with your bigger financial objectives. Whether you're saving for a down payment on a home, building your retirement fund, or creating an emergency fund, having clear financial goals can be a great motivator for making smart spending choices.

In the end, mastering the art of managing entertainment and leisure spending is all about living life to the fullest without burning through your budget. Prioritizing, budgeting, hunting for deals, planning ahead, embracing frugality, sharing the fun, and keeping an eye on subscriptions are your trusty tools for making the most of every dollar you spend on leisure.

8. Ideas to Control Transportation Costs

Getting from point A to point B is a daily necessity, but it can also be a significant part of your budget. Here, we'll explore practical strategies for evaluating and managing your transportation costs without feeling like you're stuck in the slow lane.

1. Vehicle Costs

Start by taking a closer look at your vehicle-related expenses. This includes not only the purchase price or monthly payments but also fuel, maintenance, insurance, and registration fees. Evaluate whether your current vehicle is cost-effective or if it might be time to consider a more budget-friendly option.

2. Public Transportation

If you live in an area with accessible public transportation, consider its cost-effectiveness. Weigh the expenses of using public transit against the costs of owning and maintaining a car. For some, public transportation can be a more budget-friendly choice.

3. Carpooling and Ride-Sharing

Sharing rides with others through carpooling or ride-sharing services can significantly reduce transportation costs. It not only saves on fuel and maintenance but also helps the environment.

4. Biking and Walking

For shorter trips, biking or walking can be a cost-effective and healthy alternative to driving. Consider investing in a bicycle or simply using your own two feet for nearby errands.

5. Working from Home

If your job allows for it, working from home can be a great way to cut down on commuting expenses. It not only saves money but also time and reduces stress.

6. Combining Errands

Efficiently plan your errands by combining multiple tasks into one trip. This minimizes the number of journeys you need to make and can save on fuel and time.

7. Budgeting for Maintenance

Regular vehicle maintenance is essential to prevent costly breakdowns. Budget for routine maintenance, such as oil changes and tire rotations, to extend the life of your vehicle and avoid unexpected repair bills.

8. Tracking Fuel Expenses

Keep a close eye on your fuel expenses. Look for opportunities to improve fuel efficiency, such as maintaining proper tire pressure and reducing unnecessary idling.

9. Car Insurance Review

Periodically review your car insurance policy to ensure it provides adequate coverage at a competitive price. Shopping around for insurance quotes can sometimes lead to significant savings.

10. Telecommuting and Flexible Hours

Explore the possibility of telecommuting or negotiating flexible working hours with your employer. This can help reduce your daily commute and lower transportation costs.

11. Carpooling with Colleagues

If you have colleagues who live nearby, consider carpooling to work. Sharing the commute can help cut expenses and create a more eco-friendly commute.

12. Evaluate Your Vehicle Usage

Assess whether you're making the most of your vehicle. If it sits idle for extended periods, it might be worth reevaluating its necessity and considering alternatives.

13. Public Transportation Subsidies

Check if your employer offers public transportation subsidies or discounts. This can significantly reduce your commuting costs.

14. Ride-Sharing Promotions

Take advantage of ride-sharing promotions or discounts offered by various service providers. This can make occasional rides more affordable.

15. Consider Alternative Fuels

If you're in the market for a new vehicle, explore options for alternative fuels like hybrid or electric cars. These options can reduce fuel and maintenance costs in the long run.

Managing transportation costs is about finding the right balance between convenience and budget-friendliness. By evaluating your options, optimizing your vehicle usage, and exploring alternative modes of transportation, you can navigate your way to financial savings and a smoother ride.

9. How to Grasp Significance of Small, Regular Expenses

You might not give them much thought, but those small, regular expenses that steadily trickle out of your wallet can add up to a significant financial stream. Understanding their impact is crucial for maintaining a healthy budget and achieving your financial goals.

1) The Drip Effect

Small, regular expenses are like tiny drops of water that, over time, can form a mighty river. Each individual expense might seem inconsequential, but when they occur frequently, their collective impact can be substantial. Consider your daily coffee, monthly streaming subscriptions, or weekly takeout dinners – they're all contributors to this financial flow.

2) Budget Erosion

These expenses have a sneaky way of eroding your budget. When you consistently allocate money to them, it leaves less room for more substantial savings or investments. This can hinder your ability to achieve long-term financial goals, like saving for a down payment on a house or funding your retirement.

3) Lifestyle Creep

Another impact of these small, regular expenses is lifestyle inflation. As you grow accustomed to them, your standard of living adjusts accordingly. What once felt like an optional luxury can become a perceived necessity, making it difficult to cut back when necessary.

4) The Latte Factor

You've probably heard of the "latte factor." It's the idea that frequent small expenses, like buying a daily latte, can compound into a significant financial drain. By curbing these expenses, you can redirect those funds towards savings or debt repayment.

5) Tracking the Flow

To understand the impact of these expenses, you must track them. Keep a close eye on where your money goes regularly. Mobile apps or budgeting software can help you see the flow of these smaller expenses, making it easier to spot areas where you can cut back.

6) Cutting the Leaks

Once you've identified these small, regular expenses, it's time to plug the leaks. Consider which expenses are truly bringing you value and which are simply draining your resources. Cut back on those that don't align with your financial goals.

7) Redirect and Save

The key is to redirect the funds you save from reducing these expenses into a savings or investment account. Small changes can lead to big results over time. The money you once spent on daily takeout or monthly subscription services can accumulate to fuel your financial aspirations.

8) Conscious Spending

It's not about eliminating all small, regular expenses; it's about being mindful of where your money goes. Choose to spend on the things that genuinely matter to you and bring value to your life. By being more deliberate in your spending choices, you can find the right balance between enjoying life's small pleasures and securing your financial future.

In essence, these small, regular expenses have a significant impact on your financial well-being. By recognizing their cumulative power and making conscious choices about where you allocate your resources, you can ensure that your financial stream flows in the right direction – toward your goals and aspirations.

10.   Identifying Areas for Potential Savings

In the world of personal finance, one of the fundamental principles is that to increase your savings and work towards your financial goals, you must identify areas where you can cut back on your spending. It's like a financial detective's job, and it can make a significant difference in your financial well-being.

a) Scrutinizing Your Spending

Your first step in identifying potential savings is to closely scrutinize your spending habits. This means digging into your bank and credit card statements to see where your money is going. Divide your expenses into two categories: essential and non-essential. The essentials are the things you can't do without, like housing, utilities, groceries, and transportation. Non-essentials cover all discretionary spending, such as dining out, entertainment, and shopping for non-essential items.

b) Trimming Non-Essential Expenses

When it comes to potential savings, non-essential expenses are often the low-hanging fruit. Begin by examining this category meticulously. Are there areas where you could cut back? Perhaps you can dine out less frequently, reduce the number of streaming services you subscribe to, or be more selective with your shopping for non-essential items.

c) Comparing Services

Another way to uncover savings opportunities is by comparing service providers. In today's competitive market, there are usually better deals available for utilities, insurance, and subscriptions. Review your contracts regularly and consider switching to more cost-effective options when it makes sense.

d) Energy Efficiency

Energy bills can be a substantial part of your monthly expenses. However, you can make significant savings by adopting energy-saving practices at home. Small changes like using LED bulbs, sealing drafts, and being mindful of your thermostat settings can translate into considerable savings over time.

e) Smart Grocery Shopping

Groceries are another area where you can cut costs. Plan your meals, create shopping lists, and be attentive to sale items and discounts. By avoiding impulse purchases and focusing on necessities, you can effectively reduce your grocery bills.

f)   Refinancing Debt

If you have outstanding loans, especially high-interest credit card debt, explore options for refinancing. Transferring balances to a lower-interest credit card or consolidating loans can lead to substantial savings on interest payments.

g)   Digital Subscriptions

Review your digital subscriptions. Chances are you have more streaming services or online memberships than you actively use. Consider canceling those that don't provide significant value to you.

h)   Unused Memberships

Gym memberships, magazine subscriptions, or club memberships that you hardly use can be draining your resources. Assess whether these are worth the cost or if it's time to terminate them.

i) Evaluate Transportation Costs

Your transportation costs, including vehicle-related expenses, can consume a significant portion of your budget. Consider alternatives like carpooling or public transportation, especially if they are convenient options in your area.

j) Insurance Quotes

Insurance costs can vary widely among providers. Request quotes from different insurers and compare coverage and premiums to identify a more cost-effective option.

k) Eating Ou

Frequent dining out or ordering takeout can quickly add up. Reducing the frequency of these indulgences can free up considerable funds for savings or debt reduction.

l) Unused Assets

Take stock of unused or underutilized assets in your life, like a spare room, a garage, or items you rarely use. Consider ways to monetize them, such as renting out the room on Airbnb, offering storage space, or selling items you no longer need.

m) Gifts and Special Occasions

Plan for gifts and special occasions with a predefined budget. Shop strategically to avoid overspending on birthdays, holidays, and other celebrations.

n) Financial Advisor Review

Consider consulting a financial advisor to review your investment and savings strategies. They can help you optimize your approach and identify opportunities for cost reduction.

The process of identifying areas for potential savings is an ongoing one. Regularly review your finances, set saving goals, and be proactive in searching for ways to cut expenses without sacrificing your quality of life. With careful attention and prudent choices, you can accumulate substantial savings over time, reinforcing your financial future.

11.   Strategies for Cutting Non-Essential Spending

It's a game-changer when it comes to hitting your financial goals. No rocket science here, just practical moves to make your money work smarter:

Budget Check: Start by giving your budget a good once-over. See where the cash flows in, where it's gotta go for essentials, and where it's been sneaking away to non-essentials.

Set Limits: For things like eating out, entertainment, and shopping, set yourself a budget. When you hit that limit, no more spending in those categories for the month. It's like a financial stop sign.

List It Up: Before you hit the store, whip up a shopping list. Stick to it like glue and avoid those sneaky impulse buys. A list can save your wallet and reduce waste.

Wait It Out: Got that itch for a non-essential buy? Wait. Give it a day, a week, whatever. It helps you sort needs from "I want it now" wants.

Value Over Price: It's not just about the price tag. Sometimes spending a bit more for quality or something that lasts longer can save you moolah in the long run.

Subscriptions Scrutiny: Check your subscriptions, both digital and physical. If you're not using them or they're not adding value, cut 'em loose. More cash for important stuff or saving.

Discount Detective: Before you splash out on big purchases, do your homework. Hunt for deals, discounts, and cashback offers. It's like getting paid for shopping.

Kitchen Adventure: Dining out and takeout can be budget-busters. Plan your meals, whip up some grub at home, and pack your lunch. It's cheaper and often healthier.

Second-Hand Savvy: Consider snagging some second-hand gems. Thrift stores, online marketplaces, and consignment shops can be treasure troves for clothes, furniture, and more.

Cash It Out: Cash envelope system – it's old-school but can be gold. Set a limit for non-essential spending, in cash. When the cash is gone, the spending stops till next month.

Sale Temptations: Sales and discounts might seem sweet, but they can lure you into spending on stuff you don't need. Don't fall for the hype unless it's the real deal for you.

Track and Hack: Keep an eye on your spending. Apps, spreadsheets, whatever floats your boat. Analyze your habits and spot where you can cut back further.

Be Content: Be cool with what you've got. You don't need to keep up with the Joneses or chase the latest trends. Contentment can seriously slash non-essential spending.

No-Spend Challenge: Try a "no-spend" month. It's like a financial detox. Commit to spending only on must-haves and see how much you can stash away.

Accountability Buddy: Share your money goals with a trusted friend or family member. Having someone in the know can help you stick to your plans and keep that wallet in check.

Making these moves might need a bit of self-discipline and a shift in spending habits, but the freedom and progress towards your goals are totally worth it. Let's roll!

12.   The Envelope System: A Budgeting Technique

The envelope system is a straightforward and old-school way to budget your money. It's kind of like putting your money on a diet, and it can help you take better control of your spending. Here's how it works:

1. Categorize Your Spending:

First, you need to figure out where your money goes. Make a list of your regular expenses like groceries, entertainment, dining out, or even things like gifts. These are your spending categories.

2. Allocate Cash:

Next, decide how much money you want to spend in each category. You'll withdraw this amount in cash. For example, if you set $200 for groceries and $50 for dining out, you'll need to take out $250 in cash.

3. Get Envelopes:

This is where the "envelope system" gets its name. Get yourself some envelopes, one for each spending category. Write the name of the category on the front of each envelope.

4. Fill 'Em Up:

Now comes the fun part. Take the cash you withdrew earlier and put the right amount in each envelope. So, $200 in the "Groceries" envelope, and $50 in the "Dining Out" envelope, for our example.

5. Spend from the Envelopes:

When you need to spend money in a specific category, take the cash from the matching envelope. If you're at the store buying groceries, use the money from the "Groceries" envelope. This way, you can see how much you have left for that category because once the envelope is empty, that's it for the month.

6. Be Mindful:

The envelope system encourages you to be more mindful of your spending. When you see the actual cash leaving your envelope, it can make you think twice about whether you really need that thing you're about to buy.

7. Adjust as Needed:

If you find that you're running out of cash in one envelope too soon, you might need to adjust your budget and take some from another category. It's like shifting your spending priorities.

Why It Works:

The envelope system works for a few reasons. First, it's simple and tangible. You can physically see how much money you have left in each category. It's hard to overspend when the envelope is empty. Second, it forces you to make intentional choices about your spending. You can't just swipe a card and forget about it. And lastly, it helps you stick to your budget because once the cash is gone, it's gone.

So, if you're looking for a practical way to control your spending and budget your money, give the envelope system a try. It's like giving your spending habits a friendly nudge in the right direction.

Chapter 3: Cutting Everyday Costs

"Cutting everyday costs" means finding ways to spend less money on your daily stuff without making life less awesome. It's like being a smart shopper and finding deals or making simple changes so you can keep more cash in your pocket.

Grocery Shopping Hacks

Grocery shopping can be a significant part of your monthly expenses, but with some clever hacks, you can save money while still getting all the items you need. Here are some grocery shopping hacks to help you become a savvy shopper:

1. Make a List:

Before you head to the store, make a list of what you need. Stick to it as closely as possible. This simple step can help you avoid impulse purchases.

2. Set a Budget:

Decide how much you're willing to spend before you start shopping. Having a budget in mind can keep you from overspending.

3. Buy Generic Brands:

Store brands or generic brands are often cheaper than name brands but of similar quality. Give them a try to save money.

4. Use Coupons and Discounts:

Keep an eye out for coupons, discounts, and sales. Many grocery stores have loyalty programs that offer savings to members.

5. Shop Seasonal Produce:

Fruits and vegetables in season are usually less expensive and fresher. Check what's in season and plan your meals around those items.

6. Avoid Shopping When Hungry:

Shopping when you're hungry can lead to impulsive, unhealthy, and expensive food choices. Have a snack before you go to the store.

7. Buy in Bulk:

For non-perishable items or those with a long shelf life, buying in bulk can be cost-effective. Just make sure you have enough storage space.

8. Compare Prices:

Don't just grab the first item you see. Compare prices and sizes to find the best deal. Sometimes buying a larger quantity is cheaper per unit.

9. Use a Cashback App:

There are cashback apps that offer rebates on grocery purchases. Scan your receipt and get money back on eligible items.

10. Plan Your Meals:

Planning your meals for the week can help you buy only what you need, reducing waste and saving money.

11. Skip Pre-Cut Produce:

Pre-cut fruits and vegetables are convenient but more expensive. Buy whole produce and do the chopping at home.

12. Look High and Low:

Stores often place the most expensive items at eye level. Check the top and bottom shelves for better deals.

13. Use Frozen Fruits and Vegetables:

If fresh produce is expensive or not in season, opt for frozen fruits and vegetables. They're just as nutritious and can be more budget-friendly.

14. Avoid Bottled Water:

Invest in a reusable water bottle and filter your tap water. Bottled water is expensive and not environmentally friendly.

15. Leave the Kids at Home:

Shopping with kids can lead to more impulsive purchases. If possible, leave them at home to stay focused on your list.

16. Reduce Meat Consumption:

Meat can be one of the most expensive parts of your grocery bill. Consider incorporating more plant-based proteins into your diet to save money.

17. Check Expiration Dates:

Always check expiration dates to make sure you're not buying items that will go bad before you can use them.

18. Stock Up on Sales:

When non-perishable items you use regularly go on sale, consider stocking up. This can save you money in the long run.

19. Use a Small Cart:

Using a smaller shopping cart can make it feel like you're buying more, which can help curb excessive spending.

20. Shop Alone:

Shopping with friends or family can be fun, but it can also lead to more spending. Try shopping alone to stick to your budget more easily.

By incorporating these grocery shopping hacks into your routine, you can become a more mindful and cost-effective shopper, ultimately saving money on your monthly food expenses.

Reducing Utility Bills

Utility bills, including electricity, water, and gas, can take a significant chunk out of your monthly budget. However, with some practical tips and small lifestyle adjustments, you can reduce your utility bills and save money without sacrificing comfort. Here's how:

1. Energy-Efficient Appliances:

Invest in energy-efficient appliances like LED light bulbs, Energy Star-rated appliances, and programmable thermostats. These upgrades use less energy, reducing your bills over time.

2. Unplug Devices:

Even when turned off, devices on standby mode can consume energy. Unplug chargers, electronics, and appliances you're not using to prevent "phantom" energy consumption.

3. Use Power Strips:

Plug multiple devices into power strips. When you're not using them, simply switch off the power strip to cut off power to all connected devices at once.

4. Seal Leaks:

Check your doors, windows, and any gaps for drafts. Use weatherstripping or caulk to seal any leaks, preventing heat or cool air from escaping, which can lower your heating and cooling costs.

5. Adjust Thermostat:

Lower your thermostat in the winter and raise it in the summer by a few degrees when you're away or sleeping. A programmable thermostat can automate this process for you.

6. Insulate Your Home:

Proper insulation keeps your home at a consistent temperature, reducing the need for excessive heating or cooling. Insulate your attic, walls, and floors to save on energy costs.

7. Opt for Natural Light:

During the day, open curtains and blinds to let in natural light, reducing the need for artificial lighting. When using lights, opt for energy-efficient bulbs.

8. Shorter Showers:

Hot water usage can significantly impact your energy bills. Take shorter showers or consider installing a low-flow showerhead to reduce hot water consumption.

9. Fix Leaky Faucets:

A dripping faucet can waste gallons of water over time. Fix leaks promptly to save on your water bill.

10. Air-Dry Clothes:

Avoid using your dryer by hanging clothes to air-dry. It saves on electricity and prolongs the life of your clothing.

11. Use Ceiling Fans:

Ceiling fans can help circulate air and make you feel cooler in the summer. They allow you to set your thermostat a bit higher.

12. Limit Space Heater Use:

Space heaters are energy hogs. Use them sparingly and only in the rooms you're occupying.

13. Turn Off Lights:

Get into the habit of turning off lights when you leave a room. Consider using motion-activated sensors in less frequently used spaces.

14. Cook Efficiently:

When cooking, use lids on pots and pans to cook food faster. Also, match the pot size to the burner to avoid wasting heat.

15. Time Your Showers:

Use a timer to limit your time in the shower. This not only conserves water but also reduces the energy needed to heat it.

16. Maintain Appliances:

Regularly clean and maintain appliances like refrigerators and air conditioners. Dirty appliances have to work harder, using more energy.

17. Solar Panels:

If feasible, consider installing solar panels on your property to generate your own electricity. Over time, this can significantly reduce your energy bills.

18. Water-Saving Fixtures:

Install low-flow faucets and showerheads, and consider a dual-flush toilet to reduce water consumption.

19. Air Dry Dishes:

If you have a dishwasher, use the air-dry setting rather than the heat-dry option to save on electricity.

20. Time-of-Use Plans:

Check if your utility offers time-of-use plans, where you pay less for electricity during off-peak hours. Try to schedule energy-intensive activities during these times.

By implementing these energy-saving practices, you can make a noticeable difference in your utility bills and reduce your environmental footprint, all while maintaining a comfortable and efficient home.

Transportation Savings

Transportation costs, including fuel, maintenance, and vehicle expenses, can eat into your budget. However, there are several strategies you can employ to reduce your transportation expenses and save money. Here's how:

1. Carpooling:

Consider carpooling with friends, family, or coworkers to share fuel and maintenance costs. Carpooling reduces the number of vehicles on the road and can save you money on gas.

2. Use Public Transportation:

If available, use public transportation like buses or trains for your daily commute. Public transport is often more cost-effective than driving your own vehicle, especially in areas with heavy traffic.

3. Walk or Bike:

For short distances, consider walking or biking instead of driving. This not only saves money but also promotes a healthy and eco-friendly lifestyle.

4. Car Maintenance:

Regularly maintain your vehicle to prevent costly repairs in the future. This includes oil changes, tire rotations, and brake checks.

5. Drive Efficiently:

Adopt fuel-efficient driving habits such as reducing idling time, maintaining a steady speed, and avoiding rapid acceleration. These practices can significantly improve your gas mileage.

6. Comparison Shop for Gas:

Keep an eye on gas prices and shop around for the best deals in your area. Utilize apps or websites to find the cheapest gas stations.

7. Consider a Fuel-Efficient Vehicle:

If you're in the market for a new car, opt for a fuel-efficient or hybrid vehicle. These options can save you a substantial amount on fuel costs over time.

8. Reduce Unnecessary Trips:

Plan your trips efficiently to avoid unnecessary journeys. Combining errands into one outing can reduce your overall driving.

9. Car Insurance:

Shop around for car insurance to find the best rates and discounts. Many insurers offer discounts for safe driving, multiple policies, or good student discounts.

10. Use Ride-Sharing Services:

If you live in an urban area with ride-sharing services like Uber or Lyft, consider using them for occasional trips instead of owning a car.

11. Evaluate Car Ownership:

If you live in a city with excellent public transportation, consider whether you truly need to own a car. Selling your vehicle could save you money on insurance, maintenance, and fuel.

12. Carpool Apps:

Use carpooling apps and websites to find potential carpool partners, making it easier to share rides with others in your area.

13. Commute Alternatives:

Explore alternative commuting options such as telecommuting, flexible work hours, or compressed workweeks to reduce your weekly commute expenses.

14. Maintain a Fuel Log:

Track your fuel consumption and expenses by keeping a fuel log. This can help you identify trends and make adjustments to improve fuel efficiency.

15. Reduce Vehicle Weight:

Clear your car of unnecessary items to reduce weight. Excess weight can decrease fuel efficiency.

16. Plan Routes:

Plan your routes ahead of time to avoid traffic congestion and find the shortest path to your destination.

17. Car Share Programs:

In some urban areas, car-sharing programs allow you to rent a vehicle for short periods, which can be a cost-effective alternative to owning a car.

18. Carpool Lane:

If you have passengers, use carpool lanes where available. These lanes often provide faster routes and can save you time and money.

19. Consider Hybrid or Electric Vehicles:

If feasible, consider upgrading to a hybrid or electric vehicle. These options can save you money on fuel and may offer tax incentives.

20. Shop for Auto Loans:

If you're financing your vehicle, shop for competitive auto loan rates to save on interest charges over the life of the loan.

By adopting these transportation savings strategies, you can effectively cut your commuting costs and reduce the financial burden of owning and operating a vehicle. Additionally, you'll contribute to a greener and more sustainable environment by reducing your carbon footprint.

Frugal Living Strategies

Frugal living is all about making smart choices to maximize your resources while minimizing unnecessary expenses. By adopting frugal living strategies, you can significantly reduce your spending and save money. Here are some practical ways to embrace a frugal lifestyle:

1. Budgeting:

Create a detailed budget to track your income and expenses. Knowing where your money is going is the first step in making informed financial decisions.

2. Cut Unnecessary Expenses:

Review your expenses and identify items you can cut or reduce. This might include unused subscriptions, dining out less, or finding cheaper alternatives for certain products or services.

3. Meal Planning:

Plan your meals in advance, create shopping lists, and cook at home. This not only saves money but also reduces food waste.

4. Buy Generic Brands:

Opt for store-brand or generic products instead of name brands. They often offer the same quality at a lower cost.

5. Thrift Shopping:

Explore thrift stores for clothing, furniture, and household items. You can find quality items at a fraction of the cost.

6. Use Coupons and Cashback Offers:

Look for coupons, discounts, and cashback offers when shopping online or in stores. Many apps and websites offer these savings opportunities.

7. Avoid Impulse Purchases:

Practice mindful spending by avoiding impulse purchases. Ask yourself if you genuinely need an item before buying it.

8. Limit Dining Out:

Reduce the frequency of dining out or ordering takeout. Cooking at home is typically more affordable and healthier.

9. DIY Projects:

Embrace do-it-yourself (DIY) projects for home repairs, crafting, or even gardening. DIY can save you money and provide a sense of accomplishment.

10. Save Energy:

Conserve energy by turning off lights, unplugging devices, and using energy-efficient appliances and light bulbs. Lowering your utility bills can lead to significant savings.

11. Declutter and Sell:

Selling items you no longer need or use can provide extra income. Decluttering also helps you appreciate what you have.

12. Reusable Items:

Use reusable items like water bottles, shopping bags, and cloth napkins to reduce the need for disposable products.

13. Cancel Unused Subscriptions:

Regularly review your subscriptions to streaming services, magazines, or gym memberships. Cancel those you no longer use or need.

14. Embrace Minimalism:

Adopt a minimalist mindset by focusing on what truly adds value to your life. Let go of excess possessions and unnecessary purchases.

15. Repair Before Replacing:

Before buying a new item, explore options for repairing or refurbishing what you already have.

16. Barter and Trade:

Consider bartering or trading goods or services with friends or neighbors. This can help you acquire what you need without spending money.

17. Shop Sales and Clearance:

Take advantage of sales, clearance sections, and discount stores to find bargains on a wide range of products.

18. Use Public Transportation:

If possible, use public transportation instead of owning a car to save on fuel, maintenance, and insurance costs.

19. Buy in Bulk:

Purchase non-perishable items in bulk to take advantage of lower unit prices. Be mindful of storage and expiration dates.

20. Emergency Fund:

Build an emergency fund to cover unexpected expenses, reducing the need to rely on credit or loans.

Frugal living is about making conscious choices to live within your means and prioritize savings. By implementing these strategies, you can achieve your financial goals and lead a more financially secure and sustainable life.

Chapter 4: Debt Management and Reduction

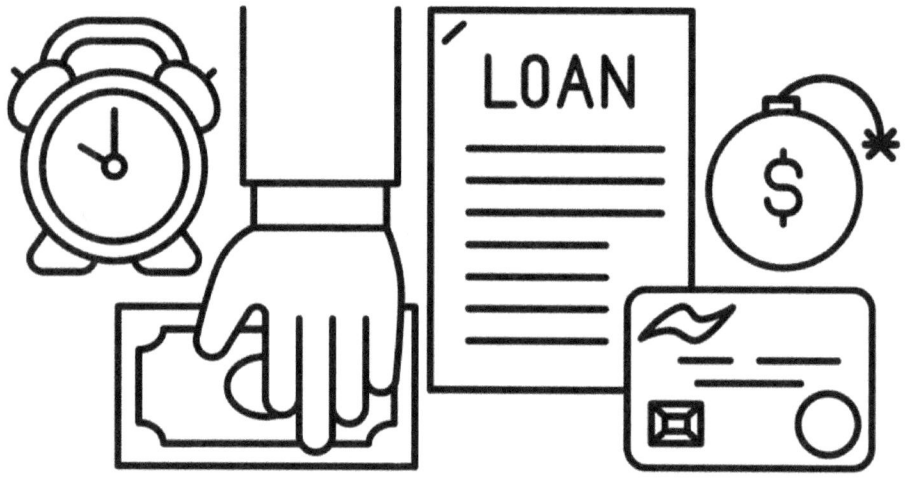

Strategies for Paying off Debt

Paying off debt is a crucial step in achieving financial freedom and reducing financial stress. Here are some effective strategies to help you become debt-free:

1. Create a Debt Payoff Plan

Start by listing all your debts, including the outstanding balance, interest rate, and minimum monthly payment. Organize your debts from the highest interest rate to the lowest. This plan helps you see the big picture and prioritize your repayments.

2. Snowball Method

The snowball method involves paying off your smallest debt first while making minimum payments on the others. Once the smallest debt is paid off, apply the amount you were paying to the next smallest debt. This method provides a psychological boost as you see quick wins.

3. Avalanche Method

The avalanche method focuses on paying off high-interest debt first, regardless of the debt amount. By targeting the debt with the highest interest rate, you can save money in the long run.

4. Debt Consolidation

Consider consolidating your debts into a single, lower-interest loan, such as a personal loan or a balance transfer credit card. This simplifies your payments and may reduce your interest costs.

5. Refinance Loans

If you have high-interest loans, look into refinancing options for lower interest rates. Mortgage refinancing, student loan refinancing, or auto loan refinancing can save you money.

6. Increase Income

Boost your income by taking on a part-time job, freelancing, or selling items you no longer need. Use the extra income to accelerate your debt payments.

7. Cut Expenses

Review your budget and find areas where you can cut back on expenses. Redirect the money you save toward debt repayment.

8. Negotiate Interest Rates

Contact your creditors to negotiate lower interest rates. Explain your situation and ask for a reduced rate, especially if you have a good payment history.

9. Use Windfalls

Use any windfalls, such as tax refunds, bonuses, or unexpected cash gifts, to make lump-sum debt payments.

10. Make Biweekly Payments

Divide your monthly payments in half and make payments every two weeks instead. Over the course of a year, this results in an extra monthly payment, reducing your debt faster.

11. Live Below Your Means

Reevaluate your lifestyle and make a commitment to live below your means. Redirect the money you save into debt repayment.

12. Establish an Emergency Fund

Build an emergency fund to cover unexpected expenses so you won't need to rely on credit cards or loans.

13. Seek Credit Counseling

If you're overwhelmed with debt, consider speaking to a credit counselor who can provide guidance and potentially set up a debt management plan.

14. Avoid New Debt

While paying off existing debt, avoid accumulating new debt. This requires discipline and changing spending habits.

15. Stay Motivated

Track your progress and celebrate milestones along the way. Staying motivated is essential for long-term success.

16. Financial Education

Educate yourself about personal finance and debt management. The more you know, the better equipped you are to make informed financial decisions.

17. Seek Professional Help

In complex situations, consider consulting a financial advisor or debt relief professional to help you navigate your debt repayment options.

18. Set Realistic Goals

Set achievable goals for paying off debt. Be patient with yourself and understand that it may take time.

19. Prioritize High-Interest Debt

Give top priority to debts with high interest rates, as they cost you more in the long run.

20. Automate Payments

Automate your debt payments to ensure you don't miss any. This can also help you stick to your debt payoff plan.

By implementing these strategies and staying committed to your debt repayment plan, you can work towards financial freedom and a debt-free future.

Debt Consolidation and Refinancing

Debt consolidation and refinancing are two financial strategies that can help you manage and reduce your debt more effectively. Here's what you need to know about each of these approaches:

Debt consolidation involves combining multiple debts into a single, more manageable loan or payment plan. This can simplify your debt repayment and potentially reduce your interest costs. Here are the key aspects of debt consolidation:

1. Types of Debt Consolidation

Debt Consolidation Loan

You take out a new loan to pay off your existing debts. This loan typically has a lower interest rate or more favorable terms, making your payments more affordable.

Balance Transfer Credit Card

You transfer high-interest credit card balances to a new credit card with a 0% or low introductory APR. This can provide a temporary interest-free period for debt repayment.

Home Equity Loan or HELOC

If you're a homeowner, you can use your home's equity to secure a loan at a lower interest rate to pay off your debts.

2. Benefits of Debt Consolidation

Simplified Repayment: You have a single monthly payment instead of managing multiple debts, making it easier to keep track of your obligations.

Lower Interest Rates

A debt consolidation loan or balance transfer card may offer lower interest rates, potentially reducing your overall interest costs.

Reduced Monthly Payments

With a lower interest rate or extended repayment term, your monthly payments may become more affordable.

3. Considerations

Eligibility

Your ability to consolidate debt depends on factors like your credit score, income, and the type of debt you have.

Risk of New Debt

Debt consolidation doesn't eliminate debt; it just makes it more manageable. To avoid accumulating new debt, it's crucial to change spending habits.

Fees and Costs

Some consolidation methods involve fees or interest charges, so be sure to understand the costs involved.

Refinancing

Refinancing is primarily associated with loans, such as mortgages, student loans, and auto loans. It involves replacing an existing loan with a new one that has better terms. Here's what you should know about refinancing:

1. Types of Refinancing

Mortgage Refinancing

You replace your current mortgage with a new one, typically to get a lower interest rate, reduce monthly payments, or change the loan term.

Student Loan Refinancing

You take out a new student loan with more favorable terms to pay off your existing student loans. This can lead to lower interest rates and more manageable payments.

Auto Loan Refinancing

Similar to student loans, auto loan refinancing involves getting a new loan to replace your current auto loan, often with better terms.

2. Benefits of Refinancing

Lower Interest Rates

By securing a loan with better terms, you can reduce the overall interest you pay over the life of the loan.

Lower Monthly Payments

Refinancing can lead to more manageable monthly payments, giving you financial breathing room.

Change Loan Terms

You can adjust the loan term when refinancing. For example, switching from a 30-year mortgage to a 15-year mortgage can help you pay off your home loan faster.

3. Considerations

Eligibility

Your credit score and financial stability play a significant role in your ability to refinance.

Closing Costs

Depending on the type of loan, refinancing may involve closing costs and fees, so it's essential to weigh these costs against potential savings.

Impact on Credit

Refinancing can affect your credit score, particularly when applying for multiple loans or credit cards in a short period.

Both debt consolidation and refinancing can be valuable tools for managing debt, but they come with specific considerations. It's essential to assess your financial situation, goals, and eligibility before deciding on the best approach for your needs.

Avoiding Common Debt Traps

Debt traps can sneak up on anyone, leading to financial stress and long-term consequences. Here are some strategies to help you avoid common debt traps and maintain your financial well-being:

1. Emergency Fund

Create an emergency fund with at least three to six months' worth of living expenses. Having this cushion can prevent you from turning to credit cards or loans in unexpected financial crises.

2. Budgeting

Develop a comprehensive budget that accounts for all your income and expenses. Regularly tracking your spending can help you stay within your means and avoid overspending.

3. Live Below Your Means

Make a commitment to live below your means, saving or investing the difference. Avoid the trap of increasing your spending as your income rises.

4. Avoid Payday Loans

Steer clear of payday loans, which often come with exorbitant interest rates. If you're facing a cash shortage, explore alternatives like personal loans or borrowing from friends or family.

5. Credit Card Discipline

Use credit cards responsibly. Pay your balance in full each month to avoid high interest charges, and be cautious with credit limits to prevent overspending.

6. Savings Goals

Set clear savings goals for emergencies, retirement, and major expenses. Regularly contribute to these savings accounts to prevent reliance on debt for such purposes.

7. Review Loan Terms

Thoroughly review the terms and conditions of any loan or credit agreement before signing. Understand interest rates, fees, and repayment schedules.

8. Avoid Impulse Buying

Implement strategies to curb impulse purchases, such as setting spending limits, creating shopping lists, and practicing delayed gratification.

9. Comparison Shop

When making significant purchases, take the time to compare prices and shop for the best deals. Avoid the trap of overpaying for items.

10. Avoid Lifestyle Inflation

As your income grows, avoid the temptation to inflate your lifestyle with unnecessary expenses. Redirect extra income into savings or investments.

11. Retirement Planning

Prioritize retirement planning early to ensure you're financially secure in your later years. Avoid the trap of not saving enough for retirement.

12. Seek Financial Education

Continuously educate yourself about personal finance. The more you know, the better equipped you are to avoid common debt traps.

13. Avoid Overreliance on Credit

While credit cards and loans can be valuable tools, avoid relying on them excessively. Aim to pay for daily expenses with your income whenever possible.

14. Financial Safety Nets

Consider insurance policies that provide protection in case of accidents, illnesses, or job loss. Having these safety nets in place can prevent financial disasters.

15. Debt Repayment Plans

If you have existing debt, create a clear plan for repayment. Use strategies like the snowball or avalanche method to pay off your debt efficiently.

16. Seek Professional Advice

If you're struggling with debt, consider consulting a financial advisor or credit counselor for guidance and assistance.

17. Avoid Excessive Use of Credit Cards

While credit cards offer convenience, using them excessively without paying off the balance can lead to mounting debt. Be mindful of your credit card usage.

18. Save for Major Purchases

Instead of financing major purchases with loans, save up for them in advance. This prevents you from falling into the trap of high-interest debt.

By implementing these strategies and being mindful of your financial decisions, you can steer clear of common debt traps and maintain a healthy financial future.

Chapter 5: Banking and Saving

High-Interest Savings Accounts

High-interest savings accounts are financial products designed to help you grow your savings while providing easy access to your funds. Here's what you need to know about high-interest savings accounts:

What Are High-Interest Savings Accounts

High-interest savings accounts are a type of bank account that offers a higher interest rate compared to a standard savings account.

These accounts are designed to help you earn more on your savings.

Key Features

Competitive Interest Rates

High-interest savings accounts typically offer interest rates higher than those of regular savings accounts, making them an attractive option for growing your savings over time.

Liquidity

You can easily access your funds in a high-interest savings account. They provide the flexibility to withdraw money when needed, making them suitable for emergency funds and short-term goals.

No or Low Fees

Many high-interest savings accounts come with minimal fees or none at all, allowing you to keep more of your earned interest.

Federal Insurance

In most countries, high-interest savings accounts are typically insured by the government up to a certain limit, providing an extra layer of security for your savings.

Benefits of High-Interest Savings Accounts

Interest Earnings

The primary benefit is the opportunity to earn a higher interest rate on your savings, helping your money grow faster compared to a regular savings account.

Liquidity

You can access your funds quickly and without penalties, making high-interest savings accounts ideal for building an emergency fund or saving for short-term goals.

Security

The government insurance on these accounts ensures that your savings are protected up to a certain limit, providing peace of mind.

Easy Access

You can manage your high-interest savings account through online banking, mobile apps, and in-person at the bank, providing convenient access to your funds.

How to Use High-Interest Savings Accounts

Emergency Fund

Use a high-interest savings account to build an emergency fund. Having easily accessible savings can provide financial security during unexpected expenses.

Short-Term Goals

Save for short-term financial goals, such as a vacation, home down payment, or car purchase. The higher interest helps you reach these objectives more quickly.

Holding Cash

Consider high-interest savings accounts as a place to hold cash temporarily, earning more interest than a standard checking account.

Considerations of High-Interest Savings Accounts

Interest Rates

While high-interest savings accounts offer better interest rates, they may still be lower than returns from long-term investments, such as stocks or bonds.

Withdrawal Limits

Some accounts may have limits on the number of withdrawals or transfers you can make each month. Be aware of these limitations.

Minimum Balance

Check if there's a minimum balance requirement to open or maintain the account. Ensure you meet the criteria.

Shopping for High-Interest Savings Accounts

Compare Rates

Research and compare high-interest savings account rates at various banks or credit unions to find the best offer.

Read Fine Print

Understand the terms and conditions of the account, including fees, withdrawal restrictions, and any minimum balance requirements.

Maximizing Your Savings

Regular Contributions

Consistently contribute to your high-interest savings account to maximize your savings over time.

Automatic Transfers

Set up automatic transfers from your checking account to your high-interest savings account to ensure regular contributions.

Reinvest Interest

Consider reinvesting the interest you earn to compound your savings more effectively.

High-interest savings accounts can be a valuable addition to your financial strategy, offering a secure and accessible way to grow your savings over time.

Investment Options for Savings To Grow Your Money

So, you've got some extra cash sitting around, and you're thinking, "What should I do with it?" Well, there are plenty of ways to make your money work for you. Here are some investment options to consider, minus all the financial jargon:

1. The Stock Market

You know those big companies you hear about all the time? Well, you can own a piece of them by buying their stocks. It's like becoming a shareholder. Stocks can go up and down, so it's a bit like a rollercoaster ride.

2. Bonds

Bonds are like IOUs. You lend money to a government or a company, and they promise to pay it back with interest. It's usually less risky than stocks.

3. Mutual Funds

Mutual funds are like investing on autopilot. You pool your money with others, and a pro takes care of investing in a bunch of different things like stocks and bonds. Less stress for you!

4. Real Estate

Ever thought about owning property? Real estate can be a solid investment. You can buy homes, apartments, or even invest in real estate companies without having to fix leaky faucets yourself.

5. Retirement Accounts

Saving for retirement is super important. With accounts like a 401(k) or an IRA, you can stash away money for your golden years, and often get some tax breaks along the way.

6. Certificates of Deposit (CDs)

CDs are like making a deal with the bank. You agree not to touch your money for a while, and in return, they give you a better interest rate. It's like a grown-up version of "I'll give you my candy if you save it for me."

7. Money Market Funds

Money market funds are like super-safe investments. They invest in short-term stuff like government bonds. You won't get rich quick, but you also won't lose sleep over it.

8. Peer-to-Peer Lending

You can be a money lender to regular folks or small businesses. They pay you interest on the money they borrow. Just like being a mini-bank.

9. Precious Metals

Gold, silver, and other shiny stuff. They might not do much sitting in your jewelry box, but they can be a cool way to hedge against financial chaos.

10. Cryptocurrencies

If you're into tech and feeling a bit adventurous, cryptocurrencies like Bitcoin or Ethereum could be your thing. They're digital money that can go up and down like a rollercoaster.

11. Education Savings Accounts

If you've got kids or plan on going back to school, these accounts are a smart way to save for education. Uncle Sam even throws in some tax perks.

12. Dollar-Cost Averaging

Don't have a clue about investing timing? No worries. With dollar-cost averaging, you just keep investing a set amount regularly. It's like slowly filling up your piggy bank.

13. Investment Properties

Want to be a landlord? Owning rental properties can earn you rent money and property value increases. Just be ready for a bit of landlord drama.

14. Start a Small Business

Got a brilliant idea? Starting a small business could be your path to wealth. But it's not for the faint of heart - it takes hard work and risk.

15. High-Yield Savings Accounts

These are like supercharged savings accounts. You get a better interest rate, and you can still get to your money quickly if you need it.

16. Robo-Advisors

If you're not a stock market whiz, robo-advisors can do the heavy lifting for you. They use algorithms to create and manage an investment portfolio based on your goals.

Before you dive into any of these options, it's smart to do your homework and maybe chat with a financial pro. It's your money, so make it work for you!

The Power of Compound Interest

Alright, let's talk about something that can make your money grow without you having to break a sweat – compound interest. It's like a magic trick for your savings.

So, What's Compound Interest?

Compound interest is what happens when you earn interest on your money, and then you earn even more interest on the interest you've already made. It's interest that piles on more interest.

How Does It Actually Work?

Here's the deal: You put some money in a savings account or investment, right? Let's say you start with $1,000, and it earns you 5% interest in a year. At the end of that year, you've got $1,050. Cool, right? Now, in the second year, you don't just earn interest on your initial $1,000; you earn it on the whole $1,050 you've got. So, at the end of year two, you're looking at $1,102.50.

Why's It a Big Deal?

The beauty of compound interest is that it can turn small savings into a pile of cash over time. It's like a snowball rolling downhill – it starts small but keeps getting bigger and faster. The longer you let it roll, the bigger the snowball.

Real-Life Example:

Imagine you start putting away $200 a month in a retirement account at age 25 and do it until you're 65. If your investments grow at an average rate of 7% each year (which is very doable), you'd have about $362,000 waiting for you. But if you put it off until you're 35, you'd only have around $160,000. That's the power of getting started early.

How to Make Compound Interest Work for You

Start saving and investing early – don't procrastinate. Time is your secret weapon.

Stay consistent. Keep putting money into your savings or investments. More money in equals more money out.

Choose investments that can tap into compound interest, like stocks or mutual funds. They have a history of delivering higher returns over time.

So, whether you're saving for your dream home, that once-in-a-lifetime trip, or just a comfy retirement, remember that compound interest can help you reach your goals faster. It's like your money working smarter, not harder. So, get that snowball rolling!

Chapter 6: Smart Shopping and Bargain Hunting

Thrift Store and Secondhand Shopping

Alright, who doesn't love a good bargain? Thrift stores and secondhand shopping are like treasure hunts for the budget-conscious. Let's dive into the world of pre-loved goodies and discover why they're a smart choice.

Why Go Thrifting?

First off, it's all about saving money. You can score fantastic items at a fraction of their original cost. That designer jacket you've been eyeing? You might find it for a steal.

It's eco-friendly. Buying secondhand means less demand for new stuff, which is great for our planet. You're reducing waste and saving resources.

Unique finds. Thrift stores are a goldmine for one-of-a-kind items. Vintage tees, retro furniture, you name it. You'll stand out from the crowd.

Hidden gems. Sometimes, you stumble upon valuable items for a few bucks. It's like finding buried treasure — but in a thrift store.

Tips for Successful Thrifting

1) Thrifting isn't a sprint; it's a marathon. Take your time and browse carefully. You never know what's waiting for you.

2) Check for any damage or wear and tear. Sometimes, you might need to do a little DIY, which can be part of the fun.

3) Sizing can be inconsistent, especially with vintage items. Know your measurements to avoid disappointment.

4) It's easy to get carried away with the great deals, so set a spending limit.

5) Thrift stores have new items all the time. Frequent visits increase your chances of finding hidden treasures.

Online Secondhand Shopping

Don't forget about online platforms. Websites and apps like eBay, Poshmark, and Facebook Marketplace offer a virtual thrift store experience. You can browse from the comfort of your home and find items from all over the world. It's like having a global thrift store at your fingertips.

The Joy of Thrifting

Thrifting isn't just about saving money; it's a thrill. It's the excitement of discovering something unique, saving a bundle, and contributing to a sustainable future. Happy hunting!

Couponing and Price Comparison: How to Be a Savvy Shopper

Who doesn't love a good deal? If you're all about saving money, then couponing and price comparison are your secret weapons. Let's dive into the world of smart shopping and uncover the tips and tricks that can keep your wallet happy.

Couponing 101

Coupons are like cash in your pocket. They can be found in newspapers, online, on apps, and even in your mailbox. The golden rule of couponing is to use them for things you'd buy anyway. Don't fall into the trap of buying stuff just because you have a coupon – that's not saving money.

You can double up on savings by using a coupon when an item is already on sale. That's the sweet spot. Don't limit yourself to grocery coupons. There are coupons for clothing, electronics, and just about everything. It's like a treasure hunt.

Be organized. Keep your coupons in a neat system so you can easily find and use them before they expire. Join store loyalty programs. Many offer exclusive deals and discounts to their members.

Price Comparison Pro

Before you buy, check the prices at different stores or websites. You'll be surprised at the price variations. Use price comparison apps and websites. They do the heavy lifting for you by showing you the best deals from various retailers. Sign up for price alerts. Some apps will notify you when the price drops on something you're interested in. Take your time. Impulse buying often means you're not getting the best deal. Comparison shopping requires a little patience.

Digital Coupons and Cashback Apps

Many stores and brands have their own apps with digital coupons. You can download these for extra savings. Cashback apps give you money back after your purchase. You just upload a pic of your receipt, and they send you cash. It's like getting paid to shop.

Stacking Savings:

The real pros stack deals. This means you use a coupon, shop during a sale, and maybe get cashback too. It's the ultimate triple-threat of savings.

Coupon Etiquette:

Don't be that person in the checkout line with a mountain of coupons, holding everyone up. Be considerate of others.

Follow the fine print on coupons. Some have restrictions, so read carefully.

If you're not going to use a coupon, leave it for someone else who might need it.

The Joy of Saving

Being a savvy shopper isn't just about spending less; it's about getting more for your money. The thrill of finding a great deal is a reward in itself. Happy saving!

Smart Online Shopping Strategies

Online shopping has revolutionized the way we shop, and it's not just convenient; it can also save you money if you know what you're doing. Let's explore some savvy strategies for getting the most bang for your buck in the digital world.

1. Sign Up for Newsletter Alerts

Many online retailers offer discounts to new subscribers. Sign up for their newsletters, and you'll often get a welcome discount code sent right to your inbox.

2. Abandon Your Cart

This sounds counterintuitive, but it works. Fill your cart with the items you want, and then leave without checking out. Some stores will send you a reminder or even a discount to lure you back and complete the purchase.

3. Compare Prices

One of the greatest advantages of online shopping is that you can easily compare prices. Use price comparison websites and browser extensions to make sure you're getting the best deal.

4. Use Cashback Websites

Sign up for cashback websites that offer you money back on your online purchases. It's like getting a discount after you've shopped.

5. Stack Coupons and Promo Codes

Look for coupon codes and promo codes before checking out. Some websites collect and share these codes, making it easy to save a little extra.

6. Shop Off-Peak

Many retailers offer better deals during off-peak hours or on certain days. Try shopping during weekdays or late at night to score savings.

7. Loyalty Programs

Join loyalty programs or customer reward clubs. You can accumulate points or receive exclusive offers over time.

8. Subscribe for Alerts

If you have a specific item in mind but don't need it urgently, subscribe to price drop alerts. Some websites offer this service and will notify you when the price goes down.

9. Use Incognito Mode

Did you know that some websites may adjust prices based on your browsing history? Shopping in incognito or private mode can sometimes get you better prices.

10. Be Cautious with Shipping Costs

Shipping costs can eat into your savings. Look for retailers that offer free or discounted shipping, or consider opting for in-store pickup if available.

11. Read Reviews

Before you click that "Buy" button, read product reviews. They can help you make an informed decision and avoid disappointment.

12. Be Mindful of Impulse Buying

Online shopping makes it easy to click and buy without thinking. Before confirming your purchase, step back and consider whether it's something you genuinely need or just a fleeting desire.

13. Check Return Policies

Always read and understand a website's return policy before making a purchase. It's essential to know what to do in case you're not satisfied with your order.

14. Make a Shopping List

Just like you would when grocery shopping, make a list of what you need before visiting an online store. This can help you stay focused and avoid unnecessary spending.

15. Stay Safe Online

Only shop from reputable websites with secure payment options. Be cautious of phishing attempts and always check that the website's URL starts with "https" for a secure connection.

The Joy of Online Savings

Online shopping doesn't have to break the bank. With these strategies, you can enjoy the convenience of digital shopping while keeping your finances in check. Happy shopping!

Chapter 7: Housing and Real Estate Savings

Renting vs. Owning: Making the Right Housing Choice

When it comes to housing, one of the most significant financial decisions you'll make is whether to rent or own your home. Both options have their advantages and drawbacks, so let's break down the key factors to help you make an informed choice.

Renting: The Pros and Cons

Pros:

Flexibility: Renting offers flexibility. You can easily move to a new place or city when your lease is up, making it a good choice if you're not ready to settle down.

Maintenance: Landlords are responsible for maintenance and repairs, so you won't have to worry about unexpected expenses for fixing a leaky roof or a faulty water heater.

Lower Upfront Costs: Renting typically requires a smaller upfront financial commitment. Security deposits and the first month's rent are generally less than a down payment on a house.

Cons:

Lack of Equity: When you rent, your monthly payments are essentially an expense. You're not building equity in a property.

Rent Increases: Rent prices can go up with little notice, which can make budgeting less predictable.

Limited Personalization: As a renter, you may have restrictions on personalizing or renovating the property to your liking.

Owning: The Pros and Cons

Pros:

Equity Building: When you buy a home, you're building equity over time, which can serve as a form of savings.

Stable Payments: With a fixed-rate mortgage, your monthly housing payment remains consistent over the loan term.

Personalization: You can make your house a home by customizing it to your preferences.

Cons:

Maintenance Costs: As a homeowner, you're responsible for maintenance and repairs, which can be expensive and unpredictable.

Higher Upfront Costs: Buying a home requires a significant upfront cost, including a down payment, closing costs, and potentially moving expenses.

Less Flexibility: Owning a home can make it less flexible to relocate for job opportunities or other personal reasons.

How to Decide:

Financial Readiness: Consider your financial situation. Do you have a stable income, emergency savings, and good credit? Can you afford the upfront costs of buying a home?

Long-Term Plans: Think about your long-term plans. Do you see yourself in the same area for the foreseeable future, or do you prefer the flexibility to move when needed?

Financial Goals: What are your financial goals? If you want to build equity and have an asset, homeownership may be more appealing. If you're focused on flexibility and minimizing upfront costs, renting may be a better fit.

Local Real Estate Market: The local housing market plays a significant role. In some areas, renting may be more cost-effective, while in others, buying might make more financial sense.

Conclusion:

There's no one-size-fits-all answer to the renting vs. owning debate. Your decision should align with your financial situation, lifestyle, and long-term goals. Remember that your housing choice isn't set in stone; you can adjust it as your circumstances change. Whether you decide to rent or own, make sure it's a choice that supports your financial well-being.

Home Buying Tips

Buying a home is a significant financial and personal milestone. It's an exciting adventure, but it can also be overwhelming if you're not prepared. To help you navigate the real estate landscape and make a wise investment, here are some essential home buying tips:

1. Set Clear Financial Goals:

Determine your budget and financial goals. How much can you comfortably afford, including a down payment, closing costs, and ongoing expenses like mortgage, taxes, and insurance?

2. Check Your Credit:

Review your credit report and credit score. A higher credit score can lead to better mortgage terms. Correct any errors and work on improving your credit if needed.

3. Get Pre-Approved for a Mortgage:

Before you start house hunting, get pre-approved for a mortgage. This not only narrows down your budget but also shows sellers that you're a serious buyer.

4. Hire a Knowledgeable Real Estate Agent:

A good real estate agent can be your best ally. They understand the market, can help you find suitable properties, and negotiate on your behalf.

5. Make a List of Your Priorities:

What features and amenities are must-haves for your new home? Create a list of priorities to guide your search.

6. Research Neighborhoods:

Investigate neighborhoods you're interested in. Consider factors like safety, schools, proximity to work, public transportation, and amenities.

7. Home Inspection is Crucial:

Don't skip the home inspection. It can reveal issues that might not be apparent during a showing, potentially saving you from costly surprises.

8. Don't Rush:

Take your time. Don't feel pressured to buy the first property you see. It's a significant investment, so be patient and thorough in your search.

9. Negotiate Wisely:

When you find the right home, negotiate effectively. Your agent can help you present an appealing offer.

10. Read and Understand the Contract:

- Carefully read and understand the purchase contract. It's a legally binding agreement, so ensure you know your rights and responsibilities.

11. Calculate the Total Cost of Ownership:

- Consider not only the purchase price but also the long-term costs of homeownership, including property taxes, insurance, and maintenance.

12. Plan for a Buffer:

- Have a financial buffer for unexpected expenses or emergencies related to your new home.

13. Attend the Final Walk-Through:

- Before closing, attend a final walk-through to ensure the property is in the agreed-upon condition.

14. Organize Your Documents:

- Keep all documents related to your home purchase organized, including the contract, inspection reports, and closing documents.

15. Be Mindful of Future Resale:

- Even if you plan to stay in your new home for years, consider its resale potential. It's a practical aspect of real estate investment.

16. Get Proper Insurance:

- Homeowners insurance is essential. Research and choose a policy that suits your needs and budget.

17. Stay Informed:

- Keep up with real estate news and trends in your area. Understanding the market can help you make informed decisions.

18. Enjoy Your New Home:

- After all the hard work, take time to enjoy your new home. Make it your own and create wonderful memories.

Remember, buying a home is a journey, and it's natural to have questions and concerns. Seek guidance from real estate professionals and do your due diligence. With careful planning and a clear understanding of your goals, you can make the home buying process a positive and rewarding experience.

Reducing Home Expenses: Tips for a More Affordable Living

Homeownership is a rewarding experience, but it comes with various expenses. Whether you're a new homeowner or have been in your home for years, there are always ways to manage and reduce your home-related costs. Here are some practical tips to help you save money and make your living situation more affordable:

1. Energy Efficiency:

Improve your home's energy efficiency. Seal drafts, upgrade insulation, and install energy-efficient appliances and lighting. Over time, this can significantly reduce your utility bills.

2. Refinance Your Mortgage:

If interest rates have dropped since you initially bought your home, consider refinancing your mortgage. Lower interest rates can lead to substantial savings over the life of your loan.

3. Home Maintenance:

Regular maintenance is essential to avoid costly repairs. Fix issues promptly to prevent them from becoming major expenses.

4. Shop Around for Insurance:

Periodically review your homeowners insurance. Compare quotes from different providers to ensure you're getting the best coverage at the most competitive rate.

5. Budget for Property Taxes:

Be prepared for property tax increases. Budget for these annual expenses to avoid any financial surprises.

6. Online Thermostats:

Invest in a programmable thermostat that lets you control your home's temperature remotely. This can help you save on heating and cooling costs.

7. Cut Down on Water Usage:

Fix leaky faucets and install water-saving fixtures. Reducing your water consumption can lead to lower utility bills.

8. DIY Home Projects:

Learn basic home repair and improvement skills. Many minor projects can be done yourself, saving you money on labor costs.

9. Refrain from Unnecessary Renovations:

While it's tempting to constantly update your home, think carefully before starting major renovations. Consider whether the expense will provide a return on investment.

10. Grow a Garden:

- Start a garden to grow your fruits and vegetables. Not only is it a healthy hobby, but it can also reduce your grocery expenses.

11. Smart Shopping:

- Be a smart shopper. Look for sales and discounts when purchasing home goods, appliances, and furniture.

12. Rent Out Unused Space:

- If you have extra space in your home, consider renting it out to a roommate or through a platform like Airbnb.

13. Review Home Services:

- Periodically review the home services you subscribe to, such as cable, internet, and phone. You might find that you can get a better deal with a different provider.

14. Create a Home Maintenance Fund:

- Set aside a portion of your income each month for a home maintenance fund. This fund can be used for unexpected repairs or upgrades.

15. Reduce Unnecessary Expenses:

- Audit your monthly expenses and eliminate services or subscriptions you no longer need or use.

16. Invest in Smart Technology:

- Smart home technology can help you control and monitor your energy usage and security systems more efficiently.

17. Home Sharing:

- Consider sharing resources with neighbors, like lawnmowers or other tools, to reduce the need to purchase your own.

18. Tax Benefits:

- Take advantage of any tax benefits available to homeowners, such as deductions for mortgage interest or energy-efficient home improvements.

Managing home expenses effectively requires diligence and smart decision-making. By implementing these strategies, you can create a more budget-friendly living environment and free up money for other financial goals.

Chapter 8: Traveling on a Budget

Affordable Travel Planning: Make Your Adventures Budget-Friendly

Traveling is a wonderful experience, but it doesn't have to break the bank. With some careful planning and a bit of creativity, you can explore new destinations while keeping your budget in check. Here are some tips for affordable travel planning:

1. Set a Realistic Budget:

Before you start planning your trip, determine how much you can comfortably spend. Be clear about your budget, including expenses for transportation, accommodation, food, activities, and souvenirs.

2. Be Flexible with Your Dates:

Travel during the off-peak season or consider flexible travel dates. Flights and accommodations are often more affordable during non-peak times.

3. Shop for Deals:

Look for deals on flights and accommodations through websites, travel apps, and email subscriptions. Compare prices and book when you find a good deal.

4. Consider Alternative Airports:

Check if flying into or out of an airport near your destination is more budget-friendly. Sometimes, a short drive can save you money on airfare.

5. Pack Light:

Traveling with carry-on luggage only can save you money on checked baggage fees and make your journey more convenient.

6. Stay in Budget-Friendly Accommodations:

Consider staying in budget hotels, hostels, or vacation rentals. Look for accommodations with good reviews and reasonable prices.

7. Use Public Transportation:

Instead of renting a car, use public transportation, ride-sharing services, or bike rentals to get around. It's often more cost-effective and allows you to experience the local culture.

8. Cook Your Meals:

Save money by eating at local restaurants or cooking your meals if you have access to a kitchen. Enjoying street food can also be an affordable and delicious option.

9. Plan Free and Low-Cost Activities:

Research free and low-cost activities at your destination, such as hiking, exploring museums, or enjoying public parks. Many cities offer free walking tours, which can be a great way to learn about the area.

10. Buy Attraction Passes:

- Some destinations offer attraction passes that provide discounts to popular sites and activities. Look into these passes to save on entry fees.

11. Travel with a Group:

- If you're comfortable traveling with others, consider going on group trips. Many travel companies offer group discounts.

12. Travel Insurance:

- While it's an added cost, travel insurance can save you money in case of unexpected events like trip cancellations or medical emergencies.

13. Limit Souvenirs:

- Souvenirs can add up quickly. Set a budget for souvenirs and consider purchasing meaningful items that won't break the bank.

14. Exchange Currency Wisely:

- When exchanging currency, compare rates and fees at different providers. It can make a significant difference in your overall expenses.

15. Travel Locally:

- Exploring destinations closer to home can be more budget-friendly and allows you to discover hidden gems in your region.

16. Use Travel Apps:

- Travel apps can help you find the best deals on accommodations, transportation, and activities. They often offer exclusive discounts.

17. Stay with Locals:

- Consider staying with locals through platforms like Airbnb or Couchsurfing. It can be an affordable and enriching way to experience a destination.

Affordable travel planning doesn't mean sacrificing quality or enjoyment. By being resourceful and mindful of your spending, you can embark on memorable adventures without overspending. Safe travels!

Budget-Friendly Accommodations: Where to Stay Without Breaking the Bank

When it comes to travel, accommodations can be a significant part of your expenses. However, there are various budget-friendly options that can help you save money without compromising comfort and convenience. Here's a guide to finding affordable places to stay:

1. Hostels:

Hostels are known for their budget-friendly dormitory-style rooms. Many also offer private rooms at a fraction of the cost of traditional hotels. They're a great way to meet fellow travelers and save money.

2. Vacation Rentals:

Websites like Airbnb, Vrbo, and HomeAway offer a wide range of vacation rentals, from entire homes to private rooms. You can often find accommodations with kitchen facilities, which can save you money on dining out.

3. Guesthouses:

Guesthouses are small, family-run accommodations that are often more affordable than hotels. They provide a homey and welcoming atmosphere.

4. Budget Hotels:

Look for well-reviewed budget hotel chains that offer comfortable rooms at affordable rates. Many budget hotels also include complimentary breakfast.

5. Motels:

Motels are generally more budget-friendly than hotels. While they may offer fewer amenities, they provide a clean and comfortable place to rest.

6. Camping:

If you enjoy the outdoors, camping can be an incredibly budget-friendly option. Many national and state parks offer campsites with basic amenities.

7. Host Families:

Some destinations offer homestays where you can stay with local families. This provides a unique cultural experience and often includes meals.

8. University Accommodations:

During academic breaks, universities rent out dorm rooms to travelers. These rooms are typically basic but cost-effective.

9. Couchsurfing:

Couchsurfing is a platform that connects travelers with hosts willing to provide a free place to stay. It's a fantastic way to meet locals and save on accommodations.

10. Monasteries and Convents:

- In some cities, monasteries and convents offer clean and simple accommodations at reasonable rates. They often have curfews and may require guests to adhere to certain rules.

11. Farm Stays:

- In rural areas, farm stays offer a unique experience. You can stay on a working farm and participate in daily activities.

12. Camping Pods and Huts:

- In certain outdoor destinations, you'll find camping pods or huts that provide shelter and basic amenities. They're an excellent option for budget-conscious nature lovers.

13. Boat Stays:

- In coastal or lakeside locations, you can find boats and houseboats available for rent. They provide a unique and often budget-friendly place to stay.

14. Boutique Hostels:

- Some hostels have elevated their offerings and provide boutique-style accommodations. These hostels offer a bit more luxury without the high price tag.

15. Last-Minute Deals:

- Consider booking accommodations last minute. You can find discounted rates as hotels and hosts try to fill empty rooms.

16. Loyalty Programs:

- If you're a member of hotel loyalty programs, you can accumulate points and receive discounts on future stays.

17. Check Reviews:

- Read reviews from fellow travelers to ensure the budget accommodation you're considering is clean, safe, and offers good value for money.

Remember that the key to budget-friendly accommodations is research and booking in advance. By exploring these options, you can save money on your travels, leaving you with more funds to enjoy activities and experiences at your destination. Happy and budget-savvy travels!

Travel Smart, Spend Less

Transportation expenses can significantly impact your travel budget, but there are plenty of ways to minimize these costs and make the most of your journey without breaking the bank. Here are some tips for saving on transportation:

1. Book in Advance:

Whether you're traveling by plane, train, or bus, booking tickets in advance often results in substantial savings. Prices tend to increase as the travel date approaches.

2. Use Fare Comparison Websites:

Take advantage of fare comparison websites and apps to find the best deals on flights, trains, buses, and car rentals. These tools make it easy to compare prices and save.

3. Be Flexible with Travel Dates:

If your travel plans allow for flexibility, consider traveling on less popular days or during off-peak hours. These times often offer lower prices.

4. Consider Budget Airlines:

Budget airlines can offer significantly cheaper fares compared to major carriers. Be sure to check their baggage policies and additional fees to ensure you're getting a good deal.

5. Use Public Transportation:

In cities, public transportation like buses and subways is usually more cost-effective than taxis or rideshares. Invest in daily or weekly passes for even more savings.

6. Walk and Cycle:

Exploring your destination on foot or by bicycle not only saves money but also allows you to experience the local culture more intimately.

7. Carpool or Rideshare:

Apps like Uber, Lyft, and BlaBlaCar can connect you with drivers heading in the same direction. Sharing the cost of transportation can be budget-friendly.

8. Rent a Fuel-Efficient Vehicle:

If renting a car is necessary, choose a fuel-efficient or hybrid vehicle. This choice can save you money on gas.

9. Combine Transportation Modes:

Sometimes, a combination of transportation modes can be more affordable. For instance, taking a train to a nearby city and then renting a car can be cheaper than a direct flight.

10. Use Reward Points and Miles:

- If you have credit card rewards or frequent flyer miles, consider using them to reduce transportation expenses.

11. Walkable Accommodation:

- Stay in accommodations that are within walking distance of major attractions and amenities. This way, you can cut down on transportation costs.

12. Consider Overnight Transportation:

- Some long-distance buses and trains offer overnight options. This way, you save on a night's accommodation while traveling to your next destination.

13. Plan Routes and Itineraries:

- Plan your routes efficiently to avoid backtracking and unnecessary travel. This minimizes transportation costs and saves time.

14. Local Discounts and Passes:

- Many cities offer transportation passes for tourists, providing unlimited access to public transportation at a fixed rate. These passes can be a great value.

15. Travel Light:

- Packing light means you can avoid checked baggage fees and move more efficiently. It also reduces the risk of over-packing and overspending.

16. Negotiate Taxi Fares:

- In some destinations, taxis don't use meters. In these cases, agree on the fare before starting your journey, or negotiate for a better price.

17. Use Local Ride-Sharing Apps:

- In some countries, local ride-sharing apps can be more affordable than international options. Check what's available at your destination.

By applying these strategies, you can significantly reduce your transportation expenses and have more money to spend on the experiences that make your trip memorable. Safe and budget-conscious travels!

Chapter 9: Health and Wellness Savings

Affordable Healthcare Options: Caring for Your Health on a Budget

Access to affordable healthcare is a fundamental need, but it can be a significant expense. However, there are various options to help you get the healthcare you need without breaking the bank. Here's a guide to affordable healthcare solutions:

1. Health Insurance:

Having health insurance is crucial for managing healthcare costs. Explore various plans, including employer-provided coverage, government programs like Medicaid or Medicare, and private insurance options. Compare premiums, deductibles, and coverage to find a plan that suits your budget.

2. Health Savings Account (HSA):

If you have a high-deductible health plan, consider opening an HSA. It allows you to save money tax-free for qualified medical expenses, reducing your out-of-pocket costs.

3. Telemedicine Services:

Telemedicine platforms offer remote consultations with healthcare professionals. They're often more affordable than in-person visits and can save you time and money.

4. Walk-In Clinics:

For non-emergency care, consider visiting walk-in clinics or urgent care centers instead of the emergency room. They usually have lower costs and shorter wait times.

5. Community Health Centers:

Many communities have health centers that offer a range of medical services on a sliding fee scale based on your income. They're an excellent option for low-cost primary care.

6. Free or Low-Cost Clinics:

Some organizations run free or low-cost clinics to provide basic medical services to individuals who can't afford traditional healthcare. Check local listings for options in your area.

7. Preventive Care:

Regular preventive care, such as vaccinations and screenings, can help you avoid costly medical expenses in the long run.

8. Prescription Assistance Programs:

If you require prescription medications, look into patient assistance programs offered by pharmaceutical companies. They can help you access necessary medications at a reduced cost.

9. Generic Medications:

Ask your healthcare provider if there are generic versions of your prescribed medications. Generics are typically more affordable and equally effective.

10. Negotiate Medical Bills:

- If you receive a medical bill that's difficult to pay, contact the healthcare provider's billing department and inquire about payment options or potential discounts.

11. Preventive Lifestyle Choices:

- Maintain a healthy lifestyle by eating well, exercising regularly, and managing stress. These choices can reduce the likelihood of medical issues and lower healthcare costs.

12. Health and Wellness Apps:

- Many apps offer health and wellness advice and resources for free or at a low cost. They can help you manage your health without incurring extra expenses.

13. Dental and Vision Clinics:

- For dental and vision care, explore clinics and providers that offer low-cost services. Consider dental schools, which often provide affordable dental care under the supervision of experienced faculty.

14. Compare Costs:

- Before getting medical tests or procedures, compare costs at different facilities. Sometimes, prices can vary significantly, and shopping around can save you money.

15. Join a Health Sharing Program:

- Health sharing programs involve a group of individuals who contribute to a shared fund for medical expenses. They can be an alternative to traditional health insurance.

16. Over-the-Counter Remedies:

- For minor health issues, consider over-the-counter remedies before seeking professional medical help. This can save you money on co-pays and prescriptions.

17. Financial Assistance:

- Some hospitals and healthcare organizations offer financial assistance programs to help individuals with medical bills. If you're facing a financial hardship, inquire about these programs.

Remember that staying proactive about your health and exploring cost-effective healthcare options are essential for maintaining your well-being without straining your budget. Prioritize your health while being mindful of your financial situation.

Fitness and Wellness on a Budget: Prioritizing Health Without Breaking the Bank

Maintaining a healthy lifestyle doesn't have to come with a hefty price tag. You can achieve your fitness and wellness goals while sticking to a budget. Here's how to prioritize health without breaking the bank:

1. Home Workouts:

Exercise doesn't require an expensive gym membership. You can achieve fitness goals at home with bodyweight exercises, resistance bands, or inexpensive workout equipment. Many online platforms offer free or low-cost workout routines and yoga sessions.

2. Outdoor Activities:

Nature provides a free and invigorating workout space. Hiking, running, cycling, and outdoor sports are excellent ways to stay fit and enjoy the outdoors without spending a dime.

3. Community Programs:

Check out your local community center or parks and recreation department for low-cost fitness classes, sports leagues, and wellness programs.

4. Online Resources:

Many apps and websites offer free or affordable workout plans, nutritional guidance, and wellness tips. You can access these resources on your smartphone or computer.

5. Bodyweight Exercises:

Simple yet effective, bodyweight exercises like push-ups, squats, and planks require no equipment and can be done anywhere.

6. Meal Planning:

Plan your meals in advance to reduce food waste and control your food expenses. Cooking at home is usually more cost-effective than eating out.

7. Home Cooking:

Preparing your meals not only saves money but also allows you to make healthier food choices. Look for budget-friendly recipes and ingredients.

8. Farmers' Markets:

Visit local farmers' markets for fresh, affordable produce. You can often find great deals on fruits and vegetables.

9. Discount Grocers:

Explore discount grocery stores and generic brands to save on groceries. Sometimes, these options offer quality items at lower prices.

10. Meal Prep:

- Batch cooking and meal prepping can save you time and money. Cook larger portions and freeze meals for later use.

11. Free Workshops:

- Look for free wellness workshops and seminars in your community. These events may cover topics like nutrition, stress management, and mental health.

12. Affordable Fitness Classes:

- Many studios and gyms offer low-cost or donation-based fitness classes, particularly for yoga and Pilates.

13. Online Challenges:

- Join online fitness challenges, which are often free or budget-friendly. These challenges provide structure and motivation for your workouts.

14. Use Public Facilities:

- Public parks and recreation areas frequently have free facilities like outdoor exercise equipment and sports courts.

15. DIY Equipment:

- Create your exercise equipment, such as dumbbells from household items like water bottles or sandbags.

16. Mental Health Apps:

- Maintain your mental well-being with affordable mental health and meditation apps. These apps offer guidance and support for stress management and mindfulness.

17. Hydration:

- Stay hydrated with tap water rather than expensive bottled water. Invest in a reusable water bottle to reduce waste.

18. Health Savings Account (HSA):

- If you have an HSA, you can use it for eligible wellness expenses, including gym memberships, nutrition counseling, and certain over-the-counter items.

19. Group Activities:

- Join free or low-cost group fitness activities in your community. Activities like group runs or walks often welcome participants of all fitness levels.

20. Thrift Store Finds:

- Look for budget-friendly workout clothing and gear at thrift stores or online marketplaces.

Remember, investing in your health and wellness is an investment in your future. You can maintain a healthy lifestyle on a budget by being resourceful and making smart choices. Whether it's finding free workout options or cooking nutritious meals at home, you can prioritize your well-being without compromising your financial goals.

Affordable Health Care Solutions

Maintaining your health is essential, and that includes managing your prescription medication costs. Here are practical tips to help you save on prescription medications:

1. Generic Alternatives:

In many cases, generic medications are equally effective as brand-name drugs but cost significantly less. Ask your doctor if there is a generic option available for your prescription.

2. Prescription Assistance Programs:

Various pharmaceutical companies offer patient assistance programs that provide free or discounted medications to individuals who meet specific income requirements. Check if you qualify for any of these programs.

3. Compare Prices:

Don't assume that all pharmacies charge the same price for your prescription. Compare prices at different pharmacies, both brick-and-mortar and online, to find the best deal.

4. Prescription Discount Cards:

Many organizations and websites offer prescription discount cards that can provide substantial savings on your medications. These cards are typically free and can be used at participating pharmacies.

5. Mail-Order Pharmacies:

Consider using mail-order pharmacies for medications you take regularly. They often offer lower prices and the convenience of having your medications delivered to your doorstep.

6. Pill Splitting:

Some medications can be safely split to provide two doses from a single tablet. Check with your doctor or pharmacist if this is an option for your medication.

7. 90-Day Supplies:

If you have a prescription for a long-term medication, opt for a 90-day supply instead of a 30-day supply. This often comes with a lower per-dose cost.

8. Talk to Your Doctor:

Discuss your medication costs with your doctor. They may be able to prescribe an equally effective but more affordable alternative.

9. Health Insurance Review:

Review your health insurance plan to understand your prescription drug coverage. Different plans may have different co-pays, formularies, and preferred pharmacies.

10. Request Samples:

- In some cases, doctors may have sample medications from pharmaceutical representatives. These can help you temporarily reduce your prescription costs.

11. Patient Assistance Foundations:

- Some non-profit organizations and foundations provide financial assistance for specific medications, especially for rare conditions.

12. State Assistance Programs:

- Some states offer programs that can help individuals with high medication costs. These programs vary by state, so check with your state's health department for information.

13. Coupons and Rebates:

- Look for manufacturer coupons or rebates for your specific medication. These can often be found on the manufacturer's website.

14. Consult a Pharmacist:

- Pharmacists are knowledgeable about medications and can provide advice on finding affordable options.

15. OTC Alternatives:

- For some conditions, over-the-counter (OTC) medications may provide relief at a lower cost. Consult your healthcare provider to explore this option.

16. Pill Organizer:

- Use a pill organizer to avoid missed doses, ensuring that you get the full benefit from your medication.

17. Ask for a 90-Day Supply:

- If you have a prescription that you'll be taking for an extended period, request a 90-day supply, which is often more cost-effective.

18. Flexible Spending Accounts (FSA) or Health Savings Accounts (HSA):

- If you have an FSA or HSA, you can use these accounts to pay for eligible medical expenses, including prescription medications.

19. Seek Generic Samples:

- Doctors may have samples of generic medications available, so it's worth asking if this is an option.

20. Keep an Updated Medication List:

- Maintain an up-to-date list of all your medications and dosages. This will help prevent medication errors and ensure you're not paying for unnecessary drugs.

Remember, your health is a priority, and there are multiple ways to save on prescription medication costs. By exploring these options and discussing them with your healthcare provider, you can access the medications you need while managing your budget effectively.

Chapter 10: Entertainment and Leisure

Affordable Entertainment Choices: Fun Without Breaking the Bank

Entertainment is an important part of life, and it doesn't have to drain your wallet. There are plenty of ways to have a great time without spending a fortune. Here are some affordable entertainment choices:

1. Free or Low-Cost Events:

Keep an eye out for free or low-cost events in your community. Many cities offer concerts, movie nights, and cultural festivals at little to no cost.

2. Public Parks:

Parks are not only great for picnics and outdoor activities but also often host free events, like yoga classes, hiking groups, and sports leagues.

3. Libraries:

Your local library is a treasure trove of entertainment. Borrow books, movies, and even video games for free. Libraries also host events like book clubs and lectures.

4. Museums and Art Galleries:

Many museums and art galleries offer free admission days or reduced prices. Take advantage of these opportunities to explore culture and art.

5. Volunteer at Events:

Volunteering at events can sometimes get you free access. Plus, it's a great way to give back to your community.

6. Outdoor Activities:

Enjoy nature through hiking, biking, camping, or simply taking a leisurely stroll in a park.

7. Local Sports:

Attend local high school or college sports events, which are often more affordable than professional sports.

8. Movie Nights at Home:

Instead of going to the movie theater, have a movie night at home with your favorite films, popcorn, and comfy blankets.

9. Potluck Dinners:

Host or attend potluck dinners with friends. Everyone contributes a dish, making it a fun and cost-effective way to enjoy good food and company.

10. Game Nights:

- Board games and card games can provide hours of entertainment. Invite friends over for a game night with snacks and drinks.

11. DIY Craft Nights:

- Get creative with DIY craft or art nights. You can work on a craft project or paint while socializing with friends.

12. Community Classes:

- Check out community centers for affordable classes like cooking, dance, or fitness.

13. Farmer's Markets:

- Farmer's markets often have live music, fresh food, and a vibrant atmosphere, all for free or at a low cost.

14. Groupon and Local Deals:

- Websites like Groupon offer discounts on a variety of entertainment options, from dining out to theater tickets.

15. Subscription Services:

- Consider subscribing to streaming services that provide access to a wide range of movies, TV shows, and documentaries. These services often cost less than a single movie ticket.

16. Educational YouTube Channels:

- Explore educational YouTube channels that offer fascinating and informative content on a wide range of topics.

17. Local Music Shows:

- Look for local bands or musicians performing at smaller venues. Tickets are usually more affordable than big-name concerts.

18. Discount Matinees:

- If you love going to the movies, consider attending a matinee show, which is typically less expensive than evening screenings.

19. Take a Scenic Drive:

- Explore the beauty of your surroundings by taking a scenic drive through the countryside or along the coast.

20. Historical Sites:

- Visit historical sites and landmarks in your area. Learning about your local history can be both educational and entertaining.

21. Beach Days:

- If you live near a beach, enjoy a day of sun and surf. Beach days are usually low-cost and a great way to unwind.

22. Local Festivals:

- Keep an eye on local festival calendars. Many festivals offer free entry and showcase food, music, and culture.

23. Outdoor Movie Screenings:

- Some communities host outdoor movie nights during the summer. Bring a blanket and snacks for an enjoyable evening under the stars.

24. Explore the Outdoors:

- Whether it's hiking, birdwatching, or stargazing, outdoor adventures are often free and provide a connection with nature.

25. Cooking Challenges:

- Have cooking challenges with friends or family where you each prepare dishes with a specific ingredient or theme.

Enjoying entertainment on a budget doesn't mean sacrificing fun. With these affordable options, you can have a great time while keeping your finances in check. Plus, exploring these activities can lead to new interests and the discovery of hidden talents.

Free and Low-Cost Activities: Fun on a Budget

Entertainment doesn't have to come with a hefty price tag. In fact, there are plenty of enjoyable activities that won't strain your wallet. Here's a list of free and low-cost activities to keep you entertained without breaking the bank:

1. Nature Walks: Take a leisurely stroll in a nearby park, forest, or nature reserve. Enjoy the fresh air, birdwatch, and connect with the great outdoors.

2. Picnics: Pack a picnic with homemade sandwiches, fruits, and snacks. Head to a local park, beach, or even your backyard for a delightful and budget-friendly meal.

3. Board Games: Dust off your board games or card games and invite friends or family over for a game night. It's a fun way to spend quality time together without spending much.

4. Movie Nights at Home: Skip the movie theater and have movie nights at home. Pop some popcorn, dim the lights, and enjoy your favorite films from the comfort of your living room.

5. Local Libraries: Visit your local library to borrow books, movies, and music for free. Many libraries also host free events and book clubs.

6. Hiking: Explore hiking trails in your area. It's an excellent way to get exercise and admire the beauty of nature.

7. DIY Art and Craft Projects: Get creative with DIY art and craft projects. You can paint, draw, knit, or engage in any craft that interests you.

8. Community Classes: Check out community centers for affordable classes like cooking, dancing, or fitness. Learning something new can be both fun and cost-effective.

9. Gardening: Cultivate a garden in your backyard or even in pots on your balcony. Gardening is a relaxing and budget-friendly hobby.

10. Exercise at Home: You don't need an expensive gym membership to stay in shape. Use online workout videos or create your own home exercise routine.

11. Free Events: Keep an eye out for free events in your community, such as concerts, outdoor movies, or cultural festivals.

12. Local Sports: Attend local sports events like high school or college games, which are often more affordable than professional sports.

13. Cooking Challenges: Challenge yourself and your friends to cook with a specific ingredient or theme. It's a fun way to test your culinary skills.

14. Photography: Grab your camera or smartphone and go on a photography adventure. Capture the beauty of everyday life or natural landscapes.

15. Volunteer Work: Give back to your community by volunteering. It's a rewarding and cost-free way to spend your time.

16. Educational YouTube Channels: Explore educational YouTube channels that offer fascinating and informative content on various topics.

17. Podcasts: Listen to podcasts that pique your interests. They're often free and can be both entertaining and educational.

18. Beach Days: If you live near the coast, enjoy a day at the beach. Sun, sand, and sea are the perfect ingredients for a low-cost getaway.

19. Historical Sites: Visit historical landmarks or museums in your area. Learning about local history can be both educational and entertaining.

20. Book Clubs: Join or start a book club with friends or neighbors. It's a great way to share your love of reading.

21. DIY Home Projects: Tackle home improvement projects you've been putting off. It's not only productive but also satisfying.

22. Scenic Drives: Take a scenic drive through the countryside or along a picturesque route. It's a simple yet delightful way to spend a day.

23. Stargazing: Head outside on a clear night and do some stargazing. All you need is a cozy blanket and maybe a telescope.

24. Local Festivals: Keep an eye on local festival schedules. Many festivals offer free entry and showcase food, music, and culture.

25. Birdwatching: Birdwatching is an enjoyable and low-cost hobby. Grab a pair of binoculars and a field guide to identify the local bird species.

26. Community Theater: Attend community theater productions or school plays. They often provide quality entertainment at a fraction of the cost of professional theater.

27. Online Courses: Take advantage of free or low-cost online courses to learn new skills or subjects at your own pace.

28. Food Tasting Tour: Organize a food tasting tour with friends. Each person can prepare a different dish, creating a culinary adventure without dining out.

29. Public Art Walk: Explore public art installations and sculptures in your city. It's like visiting an open-air art gallery for free.

30. Geocaching: Try geocaching, a real-world treasure hunt using GPS coordinates. It's a thrilling and low-cost adventure.

31. Pet Shelter Visits: Spend time with animals by visiting a local pet shelter. It's a heartwarming way to help animals in need and find a furry friend.

32. Ice Cream Social: Host an ice cream social with friends. Everyone can bring their favorite ice cream flavors and toppings for a sweet gathering.

33. Scenic Bike Rides: If you have a bike, explore your area with scenic bike rides. It's an eco-friendly way to enjoy your surroundings.

34. Online Gaming: Connect with friends or play online multiplayer games, which offer hours of fun without any additional cost.

35. Write or Journal: Express your thoughts and creativity through writing or journaling. It's a therapeutic and cost-free activity.

36. Declutter and Organize: Use your free time to declutter and organize your living space. It's a productive and satisfying way to spend your day.

37. Attend Workshops: Keep an eye out for free or low-cost workshops in your area, which can range from art and crafts to professional development.

38. People-Watching: Find a cozy spot in a park, café, or public square and enjoy some people-watching. It's a fascinating and cost-free way to spend your time.

39. Build Puzzles: Challenge yourself with jigsaw puzzles or brain teasers. They're entertaining and can be quite affordable.

40. Start a Blog or YouTube Channel: Share your interests, knowledge, or hobbies by starting a blog or YouTube channel. It's a creative outlet that can turn into a fun project.

Remember, a limited budget doesn't mean limited fun. These free and low-cost activities offer plenty of opportunities to enjoy life while staying mindful of your finances. Whether you prefer outdoor adventures, creative pursuits, or relaxing at home, there's something on this list for everyone to enjoy without spending a fortune.

Avoiding Impulse Purchases

Impulse purchases can wreak havoc on your budget and financial goals. That irresistible urge to buy something on the spot can lead to overspending and buyer's remorse. Fortunately, with a bit of awareness and self-control, you can avoid impulse purchases and make more deliberate spending decisions.

Understanding Impulse Purchases

Before we dive into strategies to avoid impulse purchases, let's understand what they are and why they happen. Impulse purchases are those spur-of-the-moment buying decisions made without careful consideration. They're often driven by emotions, desires, or external triggers like a sale sign or a persuasive salesperson.

Impulse purchases can range from small, everyday items to significant expenses like electronics or clothing. Over time, these unplanned expenditures can add up, taking a toll on your finances.

Strategies for Curbing Impulse Buying

Create a Shopping List: The simplest way to prevent impulse purchases is to go shopping with a list. Whether it's groceries, clothing, or electronics, having a list of what you need helps you stay focused and less likely to veer off course.

Set a Budget: Establish a spending limit for your shopping trips. Knowing how much you can afford to spend in advance helps you make more conscious choices.

Use Cash: Paying with physical cash can be an effective strategy. When you have a limited amount of cash on hand, you're less likely to overspend. Leave your credit cards at home if you're prone to impulsive purchases.

Wait Before Buying: When you're tempted to make a purchase, give yourself time to think it over. Delay the purchase for a day or even a week. Often, the desire to buy something fades with time.

Avoid Sale Traps: Sales and discounts can be tempting, but they can also lead to impulse purchases. Don't buy something just because it's on sale. Ask yourself if you genuinely need it.

Unsubscribe from Shopping Emails: Retailers often send enticing offers via email. Unsubscribe from these lists to reduce the temptation to buy things you don't need.

Shopping with a Purpose: Make it a habit to shop with a specific purpose. Don't wander aimlessly through stores or browse online shops without a goal in mind.

Question Your Motives: Before making a purchase, ask yourself why you want it. Is it a genuine need, or are you trying to satisfy a fleeting desire or emotion?

Leave Items in the Cart: If you're shopping online, add items to your cart but don't check out immediately. Let them sit there for a while. This gives you time to reconsider your choices.

Accountability Partner: If impulse buying is a persistent issue, consider sharing your financial goals with a trusted friend or family member. They can help keep you on track and discourage impulsive spending.

Practice Mindfulness: Be mindful of your spending habits. Stay present in the moment and ask yourself whether the purchase aligns with your values and long-term goals.

Identify Triggers: Recognize the situations or emotions that lead to impulse purchases. Once you're aware of your triggers, you can find alternative ways to address them without spending.

Seek Quality Over Quantity: Focus on the quality and utility of an item rather than its price or quantity. Often, investing in a higher-quality product that serves your needs is more cost-effective than buying several cheaper alternatives.

The Art of Deliberate Spending

Avoiding impulse purchases is a skill that can significantly improve your financial well-being. By being intentional with your spending and making more thoughtful choices, you'll find that your budget is better managed, and your financial goals are easier to reach. Remember, it's not about denying yourself, but about aligning your spending with what truly matters to you.

Chapter 11: Maximizing Your Income

Side Hustles and Part-Time Work: Boosting Your Income

In today's world, where financial stability and achieving financial goals are top priorities, many people are turning to side hustles and part-time work to supplement their income. These additional streams of income can make a significant difference in your financial well-being, and they don't always require a full-time commitment. Here, we'll explore how side hustles and part-time work can help you boost your income and achieve your financial objectives.

Understanding the Power of Side Hustles and Part-Time Work

Side hustles and part-time jobs are additional sources of income that you pursue alongside your regular full-time job or other commitments. They offer several advantages:

Additional Income: The most apparent benefit is that you'll earn extra money. This income can be used to pay off debt, save for a specific goal, or simply improve your financial stability.

Diversification: Relying solely on one income source can be risky. If you lose your main job or source of income, it can lead to financial hardship. Side hustles and part-time work diversify your income streams, reducing the risk associated with dependence on a single paycheck.

Skill Development: Many side hustles provide opportunities to learn new skills or explore your passions. This can be personally fulfilling and potentially lead to new career opportunities in the future.

Debt Repayment: If you have outstanding debts, extra income can accelerate your debt repayment plan, freeing you from financial burdens more quickly.

Financial Goals: Side income can be earmarked for specific financial goals like saving for a vacation, a home, or retirement.

Types of Side Hustles and Part-Time Work

Freelancing: If you have skills in areas like writing, graphic design, web development, or digital marketing, freelancing can be a lucrative side hustle. Many platforms connect freelancers with clients looking for short-term projects or ongoing work.

Consulting: Use your expertise in your field to offer consulting services. Businesses and individuals often seek guidance from knowledgeable professionals.

Retail or Service Jobs: Part-time jobs in retail, restaurants, or the service industry can provide flexible hours and opportunities for tips or commissions.

Online Businesses: Start an online store, sell handmade crafts, or create digital products to generate income. Platforms like Etsy and Shopify make it accessible to set up your online business.

Rideshare or Delivery Services: Companies like Uber, Lyft, and food delivery services offer opportunities for flexible part-time work.

Tutoring or Teaching: If you have knowledge in a particular subject, consider tutoring students or teaching online courses.

Pet Sitting or Babysitting: Caring for pets or children can be both enjoyable and profitable.

Gig Economy Jobs: Apps and platforms like Uber, TaskRabbit, and Fiverr offer a wide range of gig opportunities.

Maximizing Your Side Hustle Income

To make the most of your side hustle or part-time work, consider the following tips:

Time Management: Ensure your side hustle doesn't overwhelm your primary job or personal life. Balance is essential.

Set Clear Goals: Define why you're pursuing a side hustle, whether it's to pay off debt, save for a specific goal, or increase your financial stability.

Track Your Earnings: Keep a record of your side hustle income to monitor your progress and ensure you're meeting your financial objectives.

Tax Considerations: Be aware of any tax implications related to your side income. It's a good practice to set aside a portion of your earnings for taxes.

Market Yourself: If you're running your own side business, invest time in marketing and promoting your services or products.

Save and Invest: Use your extra income wisely. Consider saving or investing a portion of it to build your financial future.

Maintain Work-Life Balance: Avoid overextending yourself. It's crucial to maintain a healthy work-life balance to prevent burnout.

Remember, side hustles and part-time work can be more than just a financial boost. They can lead to personal and professional growth, expanded networks, and new opportunities. Whether you're paying off debt, saving for a dream vacation, or enhancing your financial security, these additional income sources can help you achieve your financial goals.

Negotiating Salary and Benefits

Negotiating your salary and benefits is a crucial step in achieving your financial goals and ensuring that you're fairly compensated for your work. While discussing money may feel uncomfortable, it's an essential part of securing your financial well-being. In this guide, we'll explore the art of salary and benefits negotiation and provide you with tips to maximize your compensation package.

Understanding the Importance of Negotiation

Negotiation is a valuable skill that can have a significant impact on your financial life. When you negotiate your salary and benefits, you're essentially advocating for your own worth. Here are some key reasons why negotiation matters:

Financial Security: Negotiating a higher salary can lead to increased financial stability. A well-negotiated package allows you to save, invest, and achieve your financial goals more comfortably.

Lifetime Earnings: Your initial salary sets the stage for your future earnings. Raises and bonuses are often calculated based on your starting point. Therefore, a higher starting salary can lead to more substantial lifetime earnings.

Improved Benefits: Negotiating benefits like health insurance, retirement contributions, or additional vacation days can enhance your overall compensation package and improve your financial well-being.

Recognition of Your Value: Successful negotiation communicates that you know your worth and are confident in your abilities. It can boost your self-esteem and professional reputation.

Preparing for Negotiation

Before you embark on a salary and benefits negotiation, it's crucial to be well-prepared. Here's how to get ready:

Know Your Value: Research salary ranges for your position and industry. Websites like Glassdoor, Payscale, and the Bureau of Labor Statistics provide salary data to help you determine what's fair.

Understand the Company: Learn about your potential employer's compensation policies and any unique benefits they offer. This information will help you tailor your negotiation strategy.

Identify Your Priorities: Decide which aspects of compensation are most important to you. It might be a higher base salary, bonuses, stock options, or flexible work arrangements.

Practice Your Pitch: Rehearse your negotiation conversation with a friend or mentor to build confidence and refine your talking points.

The Art of Negotiation

When you're ready to negotiate, consider these tips:

Choose the Right Time: Wait for the right moment to discuss compensation. It's often best to bring it up after a job offer is extended but before you've accepted.

Start with Enthusiasm: Express your enthusiasm for the role and the company. Emphasize that you're excited to join but need to discuss the compensation package.

Be Specific: Clearly state your desired salary or benefits. Use your research to justify your request.

Listen Actively: Pay attention to the employer's response. They may have concerns or counteroffers. Be prepared to address these and negotiate further.

Stay Positive: Maintain a positive and collaborative tone. Negotiation isn't adversarial; it's a discussion about aligning your interests.

Consider the Whole Package: Don't focus solely on salary. Think about benefits, bonuses, stock options, and other perks that might be negotiable.

Be Willing to Compromise: Sometimes, you may need to make concessions to reach an agreement. It's essential to strike a balance that benefits both you and your employer.

Accepting an Offer

When you've reached an agreement, it's time to accept the offer formally. Make sure you receive the final details in writing, including your salary, benefits, and any other agreed-upon terms. Review the offer carefully, and don't hesitate to ask for clarification if needed.

Negotiating your salary and benefits is an essential step in securing your financial future. It sets the stage for your earnings and can have a long-lasting impact on your financial well-being. Remember, negotiation is a skill that improves with practice, so don't be afraid to advocate for your worth and financial security.

Passive Income Streams

Passive income is a financial strategy that allows you to generate earnings with relatively little effort or direct involvement. Instead of trading your time for money, passive income streams can provide financial security and the freedom to focus on what truly matters to you. In this guide, we'll explore passive income, how to create it, and the different ways you can build wealth with minimal ongoing work.

Understanding Passive Income

Passive income is money earned with little to no active participation from the recipient. Unlike traditional income, which often requires you to exchange your time or labor for payment, passive income methods generate revenue without continuous effort.

The Benefits of Passive Income

Financial Freedom: Passive income can provide financial stability and even independence. It's a way to diversify your income sources and reduce reliance on a single job or business.

Time Freedom: By creating passive income streams, you free up your time. This means you can focus on your passions, spend more time with loved ones, or pursue other interests.

Wealth Building: Passive income streams, when managed well, can grow over time. This compounding effect can lead to substantial wealth accumulation.

Creating Passive Income Streams

There are various methods to generate passive income. Here are some popular options:

Real Estate: Owning rental properties can provide a steady stream of rental income. You can also invest in Real Estate Investment Trusts (REITs) or crowdfunded real estate projects.

Dividend Stocks: Invest in dividend-paying stocks. These stocks pay out a portion of their earnings to shareholders regularly.

Create a Blog or Website: Build a blog or website and monetize it through advertising, affiliate marketing, or selling digital products.

Write a Book or E-Book: If you have expertise or a passion for writing, publish a book or e-book and earn royalties on sales.

Invest in Stocks and Bonds: You can create a diversified investment portfolio that generates passive income through dividends, interest, or capital gains.

Peer-to-Peer Lending: Platforms like LendingClub and Prosper allow you to lend money to individuals or small businesses in exchange for interest payments.

Create an Online Course: Develop an online course and sell it on platforms like Udemy or Teachable. You earn income each time someone enrolls.

Royalties from Intellectual Property: If you create music, art, or other intellectual property, you can earn royalties from licensing your work.

Create a Mobile App: Developing a mobile app and monetizing it through in-app advertising or purchases can generate passive income.

Dropshipping or E-Commerce: Build an e-commerce store and use dropshipping to sell products without the need for inventory management.

Challenges and Considerations

While passive income is appealing, it's essential to recognize that not all passive income streams are entirely hands-off. Some require initial effort and ongoing maintenance, and returns are not always guaranteed. Additionally, diversifying your passive income sources can help mitigate risks.

Creating and managing passive income streams takes time, effort, and sometimes financial investment. However, the potential for long-term financial security and the freedom it offers makes it a worthwhile pursuit. Remember that building passive income is a journey, and it may take time to see significant results. So, start by exploring which passive income methods align with your interests, skills, and financial goals, and begin building your path to financial freedom.

Chapter 12: Long-Term Financial Planning

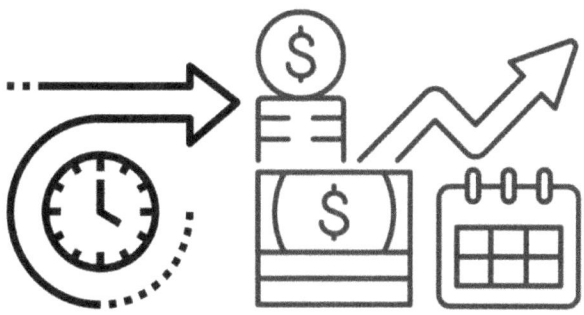

Retirement Saving Strategies: Securing Your Financial Future

Retirement is a well-deserved phase of life where you can enjoy the fruits of your labor and pursue your passions. To ensure a comfortable and financially secure retirement, it's essential to start saving early and employ effective strategies. This guide explores retirement saving strategies that can help you build a robust financial foundation for your golden years.

Why Retirement Saving Matters

Saving for retirement is crucial for several reasons:

Financial Independence: Retirement savings enable you to maintain your lifestyle and cover expenses without relying solely on Social Security or other support.

Longevity: People are living longer, which means retirement can last several decades. Sufficient savings are necessary to ensure you don't outlive your funds.

Inflation: As the cost of living increases over time, your retirement savings must keep pace to maintain your purchasing power.

Effective Retirement Saving Strategies

Start Early: Time is your most potent ally in retirement saving. The earlier you begin, the more your money can grow through compound interest. Even small, consistent contributions can lead to substantial savings over time.

Contribute to Retirement Accounts: Maximize contributions to retirement accounts like 401(k)s and IRAs. Take advantage of employer matches when available, as this is essentially "free money."

Diversify Investments: Diversification helps spread risk and maximize returns. Invest in a mix of stocks, bonds, and other assets that align with your risk tolerance and time horizon.

Automate Contributions: Set up automatic transfers from your paycheck or bank account to your retirement savings. This ensures consistent savings without the temptation to spend the money.

Catch-Up Contributions: If you're over 50, take advantage of catch-up contributions allowed by retirement accounts. This allows you to contribute more and make up for lost time.

Budget and Cut Unnecessary Expenses: Create a budget to track your spending and identify areas where you can cut back. Redirect these savings into your retirement accounts.

Avoid Early Withdrawals: Minimize early withdrawals from retirement accounts, as they can result in penalties and reduce your overall savings. Instead, explore alternative funding sources for emergencies.

Consider Roth Accounts: Roth IRAs and Roth 401(k)s offer tax-free withdrawals in retirement. Diversifying between traditional and Roth accounts can provide tax advantages in retirement.

Professional Guidance: Consult a financial advisor or planner to develop a personalized retirement savings strategy. They can help you make informed investment decisions and create a plan tailored to your goals.

Regularly Review and Adjust: Your financial situation and goals may change over time. Regularly review and adjust your retirement savings strategy to stay on track.

Social Security Planning: Understand how Social Security benefits work and the best time to start collecting them based on your circumstances.

Debt Management: Minimize high-interest debt, as it can impede your ability to save for retirement. Focus on paying off credit card debt and loans.

Challenges and Considerations

It's essential to acknowledge potential challenges in retirement saving:

Inflation: Account for the impact of inflation on your purchasing power in retirement. Consider investments that provide potential growth to combat inflation.

Healthcare Costs: Healthcare expenses can be substantial in retirement. Include these costs in your planning and explore insurance options.

Longevity Risk: Plan for the possibility of a longer retirement. Ensure your savings can sustain you throughout your lifetime.

Market Volatility: Investments can fluctuate with market conditions. Diversification and a long-term perspective can help mitigate this risk.

Retirement saving is a journey that requires discipline and commitment. By following these strategies and staying informed, you can build a secure financial future and enjoy your retirement years with confidence and peace of mind. Remember that every step you take today brings you closer to a financially secure and fulfilling retirement.

Investing for the Future

Investing is a powerful tool for growing your wealth and achieving long-term financial security. Whether you're saving for retirement, a major purchase, or simply looking to increase your net worth, effective investing can make your financial goals a reality. This guide explores the fundamentals of investing and provides insights on how to grow your wealth over time.

Why Investing Matters

Investing is essential for several reasons:

Wealth Growth: Investing offers the potential for your money to grow over time through returns and compounding.

Financial Goals: Whether it's buying a home, sending your children to college, or retiring comfortably, investing can help you achieve your financial objectives.

Inflation Protection: Investing can outpace inflation, preserving your purchasing power and ensuring your money remains valuable in the future.

Financial Security: Building a diversified investment portfolio can provide you with a safety net in times of unexpected expenses or emergencies.

Effective Investing Strategies

Start Early: The power of compounding means that the sooner you start investing, the more your money can grow. Time is one of your most valuable assets in investing.

Define Your Goals: Determine your investment goals, whether it's short-term goals like buying a home or long-term goals like retirement. Your goals will shape your investment strategy.

Diversification: Spread your investments across various asset classes, such as stocks, bonds, real estate, and even alternative investments. Diversification reduces risk and increases the potential for consistent returns.

Risk Tolerance: Assess your risk tolerance to determine the right mix of investments for your comfort level. Riskier investments may offer higher returns but come with increased volatility.

Regular Contributions: Consistently contribute to your investment portfolio, even if it's a small amount. Regular contributions help your investments grow over time.

Avoid Emotional Decisions: Emotional reactions to market volatility can lead to poor investment decisions. Stick to your long-term plan and avoid impulsive buying or selling.

Stay Informed: Keep up with financial news and market trends to make informed investment choices. Consider seeking professional advice if you're unsure about your investment strategy.

Asset Allocation: Allocate your investments among different asset classes based on your goals, risk tolerance, and time horizon. A well-structured asset allocation strategy is key to a successful portfolio.

Cost Control: Be mindful of investment fees and expenses. High fees can eat into your returns over time. Look for low-cost investment options.

Tax Efficiency: Understand the tax implications of your investments. Utilize tax-advantaged accounts like IRAs and 401(k)s to maximize your returns.

Review and Adjust: Periodically review your investment portfolio and make adjustments as needed to align with your goals and risk tolerance.

Challenges and Considerations

Investing also comes with challenges:

Volatility: Investments can fluctuate in value. It's important to have a long-term perspective and not react to short-term market fluctuations.

Risk: All investments carry some level of risk. Assess your risk tolerance and choose investments that align with it.

Market Knowledge: Successful investing requires a basic understanding of financial markets. Consider financial literacy courses or professional guidance.

Economic Factors: Economic conditions can affect investment returns. Diversification can help mitigate the impact of economic fluctuations.

Investment Scams: Be wary of investment offers that sound too good to be true. Stick with reputable financial institutions and investment professionals.

Investing is a journey that involves planning, patience, and the discipline to stay the course. By following these strategies and staying informed, you can build wealth and financial security for your future. Your investments can work for you, providing a brighter and more financially secure tomorrow.

Estate Planning and Inheritance

Estate planning is a crucial part of securing your financial legacy and ensuring that your assets are distributed according to your wishes. This guide explores the fundamentals of estate planning and inheritance, helping you navigate the complex but essential process of passing on your wealth and assets.

The Importance of Estate Planning

Estate planning is not just for the wealthy. It's a vital process for anyone who wants to have control over their assets and provide for their loved ones. Here's why it's important:

Asset Distribution: Estate planning ensures that your assets go to the individuals or organizations you choose.

Reducing Taxation: Proper planning can help minimize estate taxes and reduce the financial burden on your heirs.

Guardianship: If you have minor children, estate planning allows you to appoint a guardian for them in case of your absence.

Avoiding Probate: A well-structured estate plan can help your heirs avoid the time-consuming and costly probate process.

Peace of Mind: Knowing that your wishes will be followed and your loved ones provided for brings peace of mind.

Estate Planning Strategies

Create a Will: A will is a fundamental document that outlines how you want your assets distributed after your passing. Be sure to work with an attorney to create a legally valid will.

Name an Executor: Appoint an executor in your will to carry out your wishes. Choose someone you trust and who is willing to take on this role.

Establish Trusts: Trusts are useful for managing and distributing assets, especially when you want to specify conditions for inheritance.

Power of Attorney: Designate a trusted individual to make financial and legal decisions on your behalf if you become incapacitated.

Healthcare Proxy: Assign a healthcare proxy to make medical decisions if you can't do so. Discuss your preferences for medical care and end-of-life choices.

Beneficiary Designations: Review and update beneficiary designations on retirement accounts, life insurance, and other financial assets.

Regular Updates: Estate planning is not a one-time task. Review your plan periodically to ensure it reflects your current circumstances and wishes.

Inheritance and Beneficiaries

Clear Communication: Discuss your plans with your heirs to avoid misunderstandings and conflicts.

Equitable Distribution: Consider the best way to distribute assets among beneficiaries. Fair doesn't always mean equal.

Education and Preparation: If your heirs are receiving a significant inheritance, consider providing guidance on managing the funds wisely.

Seek Professional Guidance: Consult with an attorney and financial advisor to ensure that your estate planning and inheritance plans align with your goals and legal requirements.

Challenges and Considerations

Estate planning and inheritance can be complex and may involve challenges, including:

Estate Taxes: Depending on the size of your estate, estate taxes may apply. Consult with a tax professional to navigate these complexities.

Legal Compliance: Ensure your estate planning documents comply with state and federal laws.

Family Dynamics: Be prepared for potential family conflicts over inheritances. Open communication and a well-structured plan can help mitigate these issues.

Charitable Giving: If you plan to leave assets to charitable organizations, ensure your estate plan reflects your philanthropic goals.

Healthcare Directives: Consider including advanced healthcare directives and living wills in your estate plan to guide medical decisions if you're unable to communicate your wishes.

Estate planning and inheritance are vital aspects of securing your financial legacy and ensuring that your assets benefit your loved ones and causes you care about. By taking the time to create a well-thought-out plan, you can have peace of mind knowing that your wishes will be followed and your legacy preserved.

Chapter 13: Teaching Kids About Money

Financial Education for Children: Building a Strong Financial Foundation

Financial education is a gift that keeps on giving. Teaching children about money management early in life is a valuable investment in their future financial well-being. In this guide, we explore the importance of financial education for children and provide strategies to help you instill crucial money skills in them.

The Importance of Financial Education for Children

Early Financial Literacy: Teaching kids about money from a young age helps them develop essential financial literacy skills that will serve them well throughout their lives.

Sound Financial Decisions: With a solid understanding of financial principles, children are better equipped to make informed, responsible decisions about saving, spending, and investing.

Financial Independence: Financial education empowers children to become financially independent adults who can support themselves and make wise financial choices.

Avoiding Debt: Kids who learn to manage money early are less likely to accumulate high levels of debt in adulthood.

Setting Goals: Financial education encourages goal setting and financial planning, fostering a sense of responsibility and discipline.

Strategies for Teaching Children About Money

Start Early: Introduce basic money concepts as soon as children can understand them. Use age-appropriate language and examples.

Hands-On Learning: Give children an allowance or involve them in budgeting for family activities. This hands-on experience helps them grasp financial concepts.

Savings Accounts: Open a savings account for your child and encourage them to save a portion of their allowance or earnings regularly.

Financial Discussions: Talk openly about family finances and involve children in discussions about saving, budgeting, and spending choices.

Money Games: Use board games, apps, and online resources to make learning about money fun. Games like Monopoly or financial apps can teach budgeting and investing.

Chores and Earnings: Connect chores with allowances to instill the idea that money is earned through work and responsibility.

Setting Goals: Teach children to set savings goals for items they want, such as toys, gadgets, or trips.

Delayed Gratification: Encourage patience by teaching kids to save for a more significant purchase instead of spending impulsively.

Comparative Shopping: Involve children in shopping decisions by comparing prices and making choices based on value.

Financial Role Models: Be a good financial role model by demonstrating responsible financial behavior.

Understanding More Complex Concepts

As children grow, introduce more complex financial topics such as:

Budgeting: Teach them how to create and stick to a budget.

Banking: Explain how banks work, including savings and checking accounts.

Credit and Debt: Discuss the concept of credit, loans, and responsible borrowing.

Investing: Introduce the idea of investing and how it can help grow money over time.

Financial Goals: Encourage setting long-term financial goals like saving for college, a car, or retirement.

Economic Concepts: Discuss broader economic concepts like supply and demand, inflation, and entrepreneurship.

Encouraging Lifelong Learning

The goal of financial education for children is to equip them with the knowledge and skills to make informed financial decisions throughout their lives. By starting early and gradually introducing more complex concepts, you help your children build a strong financial foundation that will serve them well into adulthood. Ultimately, financial education is a gift that can lead to financial security and independence.

Allowance and Savings for Kids: Teaching Financial Responsibility

Introducing an allowance and savings plan for your kids is an effective way to teach them about financial responsibility, budgeting, and saving from an early age. In this guide, we'll explore how to set up an allowance system and teach your children the value of saving.

The Benefits of Giving Kids an Allowance

Financial Education: An allowance provides a hands-on way to teach kids about money, including earning, spending, and saving.

Independence: It empowers children to make their own financial choices within a structured framework, fostering independence and responsibility.

Budgeting Skills: Kids can learn how to allocate their allowance to cover different expenses, helping them develop budgeting skills.

Savings Habits: An allowance encourages saving by allocating a portion of it for future goals or unexpected expenses.

Money Management: Kids can practice managing money within a controlled environment, which prepares them for real-life financial decisions.

Setting Up an Allowance System

Determine the Amount: Decide on an appropriate amount for the allowance based on your family's financial situation and your child's age. Consider what expenses the allowance will cover.

Frequency: Determine how often you'll give the allowance, whether it's weekly, bi-weekly, or monthly.

Age-Appropriate Tasks: Assign age-appropriate chores or responsibilities that your child should complete to earn their allowance. Linking work to earnings teaches the value of effort.

Savings Allocation: Encourage your child to divide their allowance into categories, such as saving, spending, and giving. A common allocation is 50% for savings, 40% for spending, and 10% for charity or giving.

Savings Account: Open a savings account for your child. Whenever they receive their allowance, help them deposit the designated savings portion into their account.

Teaching Kids About Savings

Setting Goals: Discuss savings goals with your child. Encourage them to save for items they want, such as toys, games, or experiences.

Delayed Gratification: Teach your child to prioritize saving for larger items over immediate spending on small items. This cultivates patience and discipline.

Tracking Progress: Help your child keep track of their savings goals. Create a chart or use a savings app that shows how close they are to achieving their goals.

Rewards and Celebrations: Celebrate when your child reaches a savings goal. This reinforces the satisfaction of achieving financial objectives.

Interest Education: As your child's understanding of finance grows, explain how savings accounts earn interest, which can be an additional source of income over time.

Encouraging Charitable Giving

Incorporate a charitable giving component into your allowance system. Encourage your child to allocate a portion of their allowance to donate to a cause they care about. This teaches empathy and the importance of giving back.

The Value of Conversation

Regularly discuss financial topics with your child, such as the importance of saving, the difference between needs and wants, and the basics of budgeting. Open communication helps children develop a strong financial foundation.

By implementing an allowance and savings plan for your kids, you're not only teaching them practical money management skills but also setting them on the path to financial responsibility and independence. It's a valuable investment in their financial future.

Teen Financial Responsibility: Preparing Your Teen for Financial Independence

Teaching your teenager financial responsibility is a crucial step toward preparing them for independence and adulthood. This guide explores how to instill financial knowledge, skills, and values in your teen.

1. Financial Education

Start by providing your teen with a solid foundation in financial literacy. Cover essential topics, such as budgeting, saving, investing, and credit management. Encourage them to ask questions and seek out resources like books, online courses, or financial education programs.

2. Budgeting Skills

Help your teen create a budget. Teach them to track income, set spending limits, and categorize expenses. Emphasize the importance of balancing needs and wants, and make sure they understand the value of prioritizing saving.

3. Saving and Investing

Introduce the concepts of saving and investing early on. Encourage your teen to open a savings account and explain how compound interest works. Teach them about different investment options, such as stocks, bonds, and mutual funds, and the benefits of long-term investing.

4. Earning Income

Support your teen in seeking part-time jobs, internships, or other income-generating opportunities. This experience will not only provide financial resources but also teach them about work ethic and responsibility.

5. Credit Management

Explain the basics of credit and debt. Discuss the importance of maintaining a good credit score and the potential consequences of excessive debt. Teach them how to use credit responsibly and pay bills on time.

6. Responsible Spending

Set guidelines for responsible spending. Discuss the difference between needs and wants, and help your teen make informed purchasing decisions. Encourage them to avoid impulsive spending and think critically about financial choices.

7. Financial Planning

Guide your teen in setting financial goals. Help them create a plan for achieving these goals, whether it's saving for college, a car, or a future home. Discuss the importance of an emergency fund and being prepared for unexpected expenses.

8. Critical Thinking

Encourage your teen to think critically about financial decisions and avoid making choices solely based on peer pressure or trends. Teach them to analyze risks and rewards before making financial commitments.

9. Online Security

Educate your teen about online security and the importance of protecting personal and financial information. Teach them to recognize and avoid online scams and phishing attempts.

10. Open Communication

Maintain open and honest communication about finances with your teen. Be approachable so they can ask questions and seek guidance when needed. Encourage them to share their financial goals and concerns.

11. Real-Life Experiences

Allow your teen to make financial mistakes and learn from them. While providing guidance is essential, hands-on experience is a powerful teacher. Mistakes made in a controlled environment can be valuable lessons.

12. College and Beyond

Discuss the financial aspects of higher education, such as student loans, scholarships, and budgeting for college expenses. Prepare your teen for financial independence when they leave for college or start their career.

Teaching your teen financial responsibility is a gradual process that involves both education and practical experience. By instilling these skills and values, you're setting them on a path toward making informed financial decisions and achieving long-term financial well-being.

Chapter 14: Staying Motivated and Overcoming Challenges

Dealing with Financial Setbacks: Bouncing Back from Money Challenges

Financial setbacks can happen to anyone, and they can be stressful and discouraging. However, it's crucial to understand that overcoming financial setbacks is possible with the right strategies and mindset. This guide provides tips on how to cope with and recover from financial setbacks effectively.

1. Assess the Situation

The first step in dealing with a financial setback is to assess the situation thoroughly. Understand the root causes of the setback and the extent of the damage. Gather all the necessary financial information, including bills, statements, and any relevant documentation.

2. Stay Calm and Positive

Maintain a positive mindset. While it's natural to feel stressed or anxious, keeping a positive outlook will help you make better decisions and find solutions more effectively. Remember that setbacks are temporary, and you have the power to recover.

3. Create a New Budget

Adjust your budget to accommodate the changes in your financial situation. Reduce non-essential expenses and prioritize necessary ones. This revised budget should help you regain control over your finances and prevent further damage.

4. Negotiate with Creditors

If you're struggling with debt, reach out to your creditors. Explain your situation and inquire about possible relief options, such as lower interest rates, extended repayment terms, or hardship programs. Many creditors are willing to work with you during difficult times.

5. Emergency Fund and Savings

If you have an emergency fund, this is the time to use it. An emergency fund can provide a financial cushion during setbacks. If you don't have one, consider creating a plan to build an emergency fund for future unexpected expenses.

6. Seek Additional Income

Look for opportunities to increase your income. This might involve taking on part-time work, freelance gigs, or selling unused items. Every bit of extra income can help alleviate financial stress.

7. Prioritize Debts

Prioritize your debts based on their interest rates and consequences for non-payment. Focus on paying off high-interest debts to minimize their long-term impact on your finances. Continue making minimum payments on other debts to avoid penalties.

8. Avoid New Debt

During a financial setback, it's essential to avoid accumulating more debt. Resist the urge to use credit cards for non-essential purchases and avoid taking on new loans. This will prevent your financial situation from deteriorating further.

9. Cut Unnecessary Expenses

Identify non-essential expenses that can be temporarily eliminated. This might include dining out less, canceling subscriptions, or finding cheaper alternatives for everyday expenses. Cutting costs can free up funds for essential bills and debt payments.

10. Build or Rebuild Your Credit

If your setback has negatively impacted your credit, work on rebuilding it. Timely payments, responsible credit use, and monitoring your credit report can help improve your credit score over time.

11. Seek Professional Advice

If your financial setback is severe or complex, consider seeking professional advice. A financial advisor or credit counselor can provide guidance and strategies tailored to your specific situation.

12. Set Realistic Goals

Recovery from a financial setback may take time. Set realistic short-term and long-term financial goals. Celebrate small victories along the way, and remember that setbacks are part of the financial journey.

13. Maintain an Emergency Fund

After recovering from a setback, make building or replenishing your emergency fund a priority. Having this safety net can help you handle future financial challenges more effectively.

14. Learn from the Experience

Use the setback as an opportunity to learn and grow. Understand the factors that led to the setback and take steps to prevent similar issues in the future. This knowledge can be empowering.

Remember, setbacks are a natural part of financial life, and they don't define your financial future. By taking proactive steps, staying positive, and seeking help when needed, you can bounce back from financial challenges and work toward a more secure financial future.

Staying Consistent with Savings Goals

Staying Consistent with Savings Goals: Making Financial Resilience a Habit

Consistency is the key to achieving your savings goals and building financial resilience. Whether you're saving for an emergency fund, a vacation, or retirement, sticking to your savings plan can make a significant difference. Here's a guide on how to stay consistent with your savings goals.

1. Automate Your Savings

One of the most effective ways to ensure consistency is by automating your savings. Set up automatic transfers from your checking account to your savings or investment accounts. This way, a portion of your income is saved before you even have a chance to spend it. It takes the effort out of saving and makes it a regular, non-negotiable expense.

2. Create a Realistic Budget

Develop a budget that outlines your income, expenses, and savings goals. Your budget should be realistic and align with your financial priorities. This will help you allocate funds for savings each month and track your progress toward your goals.

3. Set Specific Savings Goals

Having clear and specific savings goals provides motivation and direction. Instead of vague goals like "save more money," specify how much you want to save and by when. For example, "Save $5,000 for a down payment on a house within two years." Specific goals are easier to work towards.

4. Prioritize Your Savings

Make savings a priority in your budget. Treat it like a mandatory expense. Before allocating funds for discretionary spending, allocate money to your savings goals. This ensures that your savings goals are consistently funded.

5. Celebrate Milestones

Celebrate small milestones along the way. When you reach a specific savings target, treat yourself to something modest. It reinforces the habit of saving and gives you a sense of accomplishment. Just make sure the reward doesn't derail your savings efforts.

6. Stay Accountable

Share your savings goals with a trusted friend or family member who can help hold you accountable. Having someone to share your progress with can motivate you to stay consistent. You can also consider joining a savings or investment group for added support.

7. Review and Adjust Your Plan

Periodically review your savings plan to ensure it remains aligned with your financial goals and current circumstances. Life changes, and so should your savings strategy. Adjust your plan as needed to keep it on track.

8. Overcome Temptations

Temptations to spend can be strong, but resisting them is essential for consistency. When tempted to make an impulse purchase, remind yourself of your goals and the financial security and opportunities they represent.

9. Visualize Your Goals

Visualizing your goals can help keep you motivated and consistent. Create a vision board or regularly picture the benefits of achieving your savings goals. Visualization can make your goals feel more attainable.

10. Stay Informed

Stay informed about the best savings and investment options. Knowledge can help you make more informed decisions and stay motivated. It's also an essential part of maintaining consistency in your savings approach.

11. Practice Patience

Consistency is a long-term game. There may be times when progress seems slow, but patience is key. Stay focused on the big picture, and remember that the financial security and freedom you're working towards are worth it.

12. Seek Professional Guidance

If you find it challenging to stay consistent with your savings goals, consider seeking advice from a financial advisor. They can offer strategies and insights tailored to your unique situation.

Consistency in savings is a powerful financial habit that can lead to financial security, peace of mind, and the ability to achieve your financial aspirations. By following these strategies and making savings a routine part of your financial life, you can stay consistent and reach your goals.

Celebrating Financial Milestones

Celebrating Financial Milestones: Enjoying the Fruits of Your Financial Labor

Reaching financial milestones is a significant achievement. Whether you've paid off a substantial portion of your debt, hit a savings target, or reached a critical point in your investment journey, it's essential to celebrate these accomplishments. Here's why and how to celebrate your financial milestones:

Why Celebrate Financial Milestones?

Motivation: Celebrating milestones provides motivation to continue your financial journey. It reinforces the idea that hard work and discipline pay off, encouraging you to stay on track.

Positive Reinforcement: Celebrating reinforces positive financial behavior. When you see the results of your efforts, you're more likely to maintain and build upon those habits.

Stress Reduction: Achieving financial goals can alleviate stress and anxiety. Celebrating helps you relax, reduce financial worries, and enjoy the present moment.

Sense of Accomplishment: Acknowledging your progress gives you a sense of accomplishment. It reminds you of how far you've come and how capable you are of reaching your financial goals.

How to Celebrate Financial Milestones:

Treat Yourself: Enjoy a modest reward for your achievement. It could be a special meal, a spa day, or something that brings you joy. Just make sure it's within your budget.

Share Your Success: Share your success with friends or family. They can offer their congratulations and support, making the milestone more meaningful.

Reflect on Your Progress: Take a moment to reflect on your journey. Appreciate the hard work and discipline it took to reach the milestone.

Update Your Goals: After celebrating, revisit your financial goals. Consider adjusting or expanding them to keep your financial journey exciting and engaging.

Create a Milestone Journal: Keep a journal of your financial milestones. Write about your feelings, challenges, and the actions that helped you achieve each goal. This journal can be a source of inspiration and motivation.

Give Back: Use your success as an opportunity to give back. Donate to a charity or cause you care about or offer financial advice to others who might benefit from your experience.

Plan for the Future: As you celebrate, plan for your next financial milestone. Setting new goals keeps you focused and driven.

Educate Yourself: Use your milestone as a reason to learn more about personal finance. The more you know, the better you can manage your finances and achieve even greater success.

Stay Humble: While celebrating is essential, it's also vital to remain humble and remember your financial journey's challenges. Staying grounded ensures you continue to make wise financial decisions.

Seek Professional Advice: If you've reached a significant financial milestone, consider consulting a financial advisor. They can help you make the most of your achievements and plan for the future.

Remember that celebrating financial milestones doesn't have to be extravagant. It's about recognizing your hard work and commitment. By doing so, you'll stay motivated, appreciate your financial journey, and continue to progress toward your long-term financial goals.

Chapter 15: Money-Saving Success Stories

Real-Life Inspirational Stories of Money-Saving Success

Real-life examples of individuals who have achieved money-saving success can be incredibly motivating. They demonstrate that with determination, smart strategies, and commitment, anyone can improve their financial situation. Here are a few inspirational stories:

Debt-Free at 30: Sarah, a young professional, managed to become debt-free by her 30th birthday. She accomplished this by creating a detailed budget, finding side gigs, and consistently paying down her debts. Her story serves as a testament to how focused financial planning can lead to remarkable results.

Retired in Their 40s: Jim and Jenny, a couple in their 40s, achieved early retirement by diligently saving and investing. They prioritized their long-term financial goals over short-term pleasures. Their story inspires others to set ambitious savings goals and make sacrifices when necessary.

College Graduate Debt-Free: Mark graduated from college without any student loan debt. He achieved this by working part-time throughout his studies, applying for scholarships, and attending a more affordable university. Mark's story underscores the importance of financial planning before and during college.

Family's Dream Vacation: The Garcia family saved for a dream vacation to Europe over several years. They set up a dedicated savings account and cut down on discretionary spending. Their story shows how family financial goals can bring loved ones closer together.

New Homeowner: Lisa, a single mom, bought her first home after years of diligent saving. She attended first-time homebuyer seminars, researched mortgage options, and worked closely with a real estate agent. Lisa's experience demonstrates how financial education and patience can lead to homeownership.

Entrepreneurial Success: Chris started a small business with a clear plan for saving money from the outset. His business grew steadily, and he consistently reinvested his profits into the company. Chris's story highlights how entrepreneurship can lead to financial independence.

Early Debt Payoff: Sarah and John, a couple with significant credit card debt, paid off all their balances in just two years. They created a debt payoff plan, cut non-essential spending, and increased their income through side jobs. Their story is a testament to the power of determination and financial discipline.

Financial Recovery After Setbacks: Tom faced unexpected medical bills and job loss, which depleted his savings. However, he managed to rebuild his finances by setting up an emergency fund, prioritizing saving, and investing wisely. His story showcases resilience in the face of financial setbacks.

College Savings for Kids: Maria and David prioritized saving for their children's college education. They started when their kids were young and diligently contributed to 529 plans. Their story emphasizes the importance of planning for future expenses, even if they seem distant.

These real-life stories serve as valuable reminders that saving money and achieving financial success are within reach for anyone willing to set clear goals, develop practical strategies, and remain committed to their financial journey. They inspire and demonstrate that with the right mindset, anyone can attain financial stability and reach their financial goals.

Inspiring Stories of Financial Transformation

Financial transformation is possible, no matter where you start. These real-life stories of individuals who turned their financial lives around can inspire and motivate anyone looking to improve their financial situation:

From Debt to Debt-Free: Maria and Michael found themselves drowning in credit card debt. They decided to take control of their finances and developed a plan to pay off their debts systematically. Through budgeting and consistent payments, they became debt-free in five years. Their journey highlights the power of determination and disciplined financial planning.

Starting from Scratch: Emily, a recent college graduate, began her journey to financial independence with minimal savings and student loan debt. She set clear financial goals, found a stable job, and focused on living within her means. Over the years, she not only paid off her loans but also saved for her future. Her story proves that even those with modest beginnings can achieve financial success.

Early Retirement: John, an IT professional, had a dream of retiring early. He saved aggressively, invested wisely, and stuck to his budget. At the age of 45, John was able to retire comfortably. His story shows that with a well-thought-out plan and dedication, early retirement is achievable.

Single Parent Success: Lisa, a single mother, faced numerous financial challenges. She juggled work, parenting, and financial responsibilities. Through careful budgeting, seeking child support, and financial education, she was able to provide a stable and secure life for her family. Her story is a testament to resilience and determination.

Business Owner Turnaround: Richard, a small business owner, faced the brink of bankruptcy. He sought professional help, restructured his business, and found ways to cut costs. With hard work and careful financial management, his business not only survived but thrived. Richard's story demonstrates that even in challenging situations, financial recovery is possible.

Traveling the World Debt-Free: Michelle and Robert dreamed of traveling the world. They set a goal to save for their travels, cut back on non-essential spending, and even started a travel blog. In a few years, they embarked on their adventure, fully funded, without accumulating debt. Their story shows that even extravagant dreams can be achieved through dedicated savings and creativity.

Retirement After Job Loss: David lost his job during a company downsizing when he was in his 50s. Instead of giving in to despair, he pursued part-time work, continued to save, and managed to retire comfortably. His story proves that life's unexpected turns can be navigated with resilience and financial adaptability.

Financial Education for the Family: The Martinez family, after facing financial difficulties, decided to educate themselves about money. They read books, attended financial seminars, and set clear financial goals. They not only improved their financial situation but also passed on their knowledge to their children. Their story shows that financial education can transform not just one life, but an entire family's future.

These inspiring stories demonstrate that financial transformation is possible through discipline, perseverance, and sound financial planning. No matter your starting point, with the right mindset and strategies, you can achieve your financial goals and build a brighter financial future.

Chapter 16: The Road to Financial Freedom

The Path to Achieving Financial Freedom

Financial independence is the dream of many, and it's not an unattainable goal. With commitment, discipline, and the right strategies, you can embark on the path to financial independence. Here's a roadmap to guide you on your journey:

1. Set Clear Financial Goals:

Start by defining your financial objectives. What does financial independence mean to you? Is it early retirement, debt freedom, or the ability to pursue your passions without worrying about money? Your goals will serve as your roadmap.

2. Create a Detailed Budget:

Develop a comprehensive budget that outlines your income, expenses, and savings goals. A budget is the foundation of your financial plan, helping you track your progress and make informed decisions.

3. Reduce Debt:

Prioritize paying off high-interest debt, such as credit card balances and personal loans. The less debt you have, the more money you can redirect towards savings and investments.

4. Build an Emergency Fund:

An emergency fund is your financial safety net. Aim to save three to six months' worth of living expenses in a separate account to cover unexpected costs.

5. Maximize Retirement Contributions:

Take full advantage of retirement accounts like 401(k)s or IRAs. These tax-advantaged savings vehicles can significantly boost your long-term financial security.

6. Invest Wisely:

Learn about different investment options and create a diversified portfolio that aligns with your risk tolerance and goals. Investments can provide a source of passive income and long-term growth.

7. Live Below Your Means:

Maintain a frugal lifestyle that allows you to save and invest a significant portion of your income. Avoid lifestyle inflation, which can erode your savings potential.

8. Continuously Educate Yourself:

Stay informed about personal finance and investment strategies. Continuous learning can help you make informed financial decisions.

9. Seek Additional Income Streams:

Explore side hustles, freelance work, or passive income opportunities to supplement your primary income. These extra earnings can accelerate your journey to financial independence.

10. Monitor and Adjust:

Regularly review your financial progress and adjust your strategies as needed. Financial independence is a dynamic goal that may require course corrections along the way.

11. Focus on Long-Term Wealth:

Remember that achieving financial independence is about building wealth over time. Be patient and stay committed to your plan.

12. Celebrate Milestones:

Recognize and celebrate your financial achievements along the way. Whether it's paying off a significant debt, reaching a savings milestone, or experiencing the freedom of a side income stream, each step brings you closer to your goal.

13. Consider Retiring Early:

If early retirement is your goal, create a plan that factors in healthcare, budgeting, and sustainable income streams.

14. Evaluate Your Portfolio:

As you approach your goal, assess your investment portfolio to ensure it aligns with your retirement needs.

15. Achieve and Enjoy Financial Independence:

Once you've reached your financial independence goal, relish the freedom it brings. You can choose how to spend your time, whether that means pursuing hobbies, traveling, or giving back to the community.

Remember that financial independence is unique to your goals and circumstances. Your journey may take time, but every step brings you closer to the freedom and security you desire. Stay focused, remain adaptable, and believe in your ability to achieve financial independence.

Setting a Long-Term Financial Vision

Creating a long-term financial vision is the first step toward achieving your financial goals and securing your future. It's about crafting a clear and inspiring picture of where you want to be financially, and then working methodically toward that vision. Here's how to set a long-term financial vision that will guide your financial journey:

1. Define Your Objectives:

Start by identifying your long-term financial objectives. What do you want to achieve? This could include goals like retiring comfortably, buying a home, funding your children's education, or becoming debt-free.

2. Visualize Your Ideal Financial Future:

Imagine your life when you've accomplished these objectives. What does it look like? How do you spend your time? What does your financial situation feel like? Creating a vivid mental picture of your ideal financial future can be motivating.

3. Break Down Your Goals:

Divide your long-term objectives into smaller, manageable goals. For instance, if your vision is to retire comfortably, set smaller goals like maxing out your retirement account contributions each year, paying off high-interest debt, and creating an emergency fund.

4. Create a Timeline:

Assign timelines to your goals. When do you want to achieve each one? Having a clear timeframe adds urgency and structure to your vision.

5. Evaluate Your Current Situation:

Take stock of your current financial situation. This includes assessing your income, expenses, assets, debts, and investments. Understanding where you stand today is crucial for crafting a realistic path to your financial vision.

6. Set Budget and Savings Targets:

Develop a budget that allocates your income to cover essential expenses, savings, and discretionary spending. Your budget is a practical tool for working toward your long-term vision.

7. Prioritize Saving and Investing:

Allocate a significant portion of your income to savings and investments to fund your long-term goals. Consider retirement accounts, investment portfolios, and other wealth-building strategies.

8. Develop a Plan:

Create a detailed plan for each of your smaller goals. For example, if you're saving for a down payment on a house, outline how much you need to save each month and what actions you'll take to cut expenses or boost your income to reach that target.

9. Continuously Educate Yourself:

Stay informed about financial planning, investment opportunities, and strategies to meet your goals. The more you know, the more effectively you can plan and execute your vision.

10. Seek Professional Guidance:

Consider consulting with a financial advisor to get expert insights and advice on your long-term vision. A professional can help you make informed financial decisions.

11. Be Flexible:

Understand that life circumstances can change. Be adaptable and willing to adjust your plan as needed to stay on track toward your vision.

12. Monitor and Celebrate Progress:

Regularly review your financial progress and celebrate each milestone. It can be motivating to see how far you've come.

13. Share Your Vision:

Share your long-term financial vision with a trusted friend or family member who can provide support, encouragement, and accountability.

Remember, setting a long-term financial vision is about mapping out the future you desire and then working diligently to make it a reality. Your vision is a guiding light that will keep you focused and inspired throughout your financial journey. Stay committed, be patient, and believe in your ability to turn your vision into a thriving financial reality.

Building Wealth and Security

Building wealth and financial security is a journey that requires planning, discipline, and a commitment to your long-term financial well-being. Whether you're just starting on your financial path or looking to enhance your current financial situation, these steps will guide you toward building wealth and security:

1. Set Clear Financial Goals:

Start by defining your financial objectives. What do you want to achieve? These goals could include retirement savings, homeownership, debt reduction, or funding your children's education.

2. Create a Budget:

Develop a comprehensive budget that outlines your income, expenses, and savings goals. A budget helps you understand your financial flow and identify areas where you can cut costs.

3. Live Within Your Means:

Make an effort to spend less than you earn. This fundamental principle is essential for building wealth. Avoid excessive debt and make responsible financial choices.

4. Save and Invest Consistently:

Allocate a portion of your income to savings and investments regularly. This includes contributions to retirement accounts, emergency funds, and other investment vehicles.

5. Maximize Retirement Contributions:

Take advantage of employer-sponsored retirement plans, such as 401(k)s, and consider maximizing your contributions to benefit from tax advantages and potential employer matches.

6. Diversify Your Investments:

Diversification is key to managing risk and potentially earning better returns. Invest in a mix of assets, such as stocks, bonds, and real estate, to spread risk and enhance your portfolio.

7. Eliminate High-Interest Debt:

High-interest debt, such as credit card balances, can erode your wealth. Prioritize paying off these debts to free up more of your income for savings and investments.

8. Build an Emergency Fund:

Set aside three to six months' worth of living expenses in an easily accessible savings account. This will provide a financial safety net in case of unexpected expenses or emergencies.

9. Continuously Educate Yourself:

Stay informed about personal finance and investment strategies. The more you know, the better you can make informed financial decisions.

10. Seek Professional Guidance:

Consider working with a financial advisor to create a personalized wealth-building plan. An advisor can provide expert insights and help you navigate complex financial decisions.

11. Invest for the Long Term:

Building wealth takes time. Avoid trying to time the market or making impulsive investment decisions. Instead, focus on a long-term investment strategy.

12. Be Patient and Persistent:

Building wealth is a marathon, not a sprint. Stay committed to your financial plan, even in challenging economic times.

13. Protect Your Assets:

Secure your assets with insurance, including health, life, disability, and homeowner's or renter's insurance. Protecting what you have is crucial for long-term financial security.

14. Reinvest Profits:

As your investments grow, consider reinvesting the profits and dividends to take advantage of compounding returns.

15. Estate Planning:

Create an estate plan to ensure that your wealth is distributed according to your wishes. This may include writing a will, establishing trusts, and designating beneficiaries.

Building wealth and financial security is a continuous process that requires patience, discipline, and a strategic approach. By following these steps, you can set yourself on the path to financial success and create a more secure future for yourself and your loved ones. Remember, the journey to wealth is built one step at a time, and every step you take brings you closer to your financial goals.

The End.

www.ingramcontent.com/pod-product-compliance
Lightning Source LLC
Chambersburg PA
CBHW072344290526
45794CB00001B/2